Alastair Sawday's

SPECIAL PLACES TO STAY IN IRELAND

Typesetting, Conversion & Repro:	Avonset, Bath
Maps:	Maps in Minutes, Devon
Printing:	Jarrold Book Printing, Norwich
Design:	Springboard Design, Bristol
UK Distribution:	Portfolio, London
US Distribution:	St Martin's Press, New York

First published in 1999 by Alastair Sawday Publishing Co. Ltd
44 Ambra Vale East, Bristol BS8 4RE, UK.

Alastair Sawday has asserted his right to be identified as the author of this work.
ISBN 1-901970-02-7 Printed in the UK

Alastair Sawday's

SPECIAL PLACES TO STAY
IN
IRELAND

"May you have warm words on a cold evening,
A full moon on a dark night,
And the road downhill all the way to your door."

Traditional Irish blessing

ASP
Alastair Sawday Publishing

ACKNOWLEGEMENTS

The remarkable part of Simon's achievement in creating another edition of this seductive volume is that he did it in the teeth of a hurricane of irresistible Irish hospitality. He seems to have struggled heroically to extricate himself from one after another deep, whisky-served, sofa only to be forced to tumble gratefully into the arms of yet another family of agreeable hosts.

Such were the perils of the job that Simon told us, firmly and on several occasions, that this was work for him only. So we could only watch from the sidelines as he fought his way through a jungle of kindness and generosity, spiced with characters that made us all feel that 'all is not lost with human kind'; the world is, clearly, alive with rich personalities and remarkable stories and this book is awash with them. It is to Simon's credit that he kept his head when confronted with so many. He has made a splendid selection and I congratulate him.

Series Editor:	Alastair Sawday
Editor:	Simon Greenwood
Production Manager:	Julia Richardson
Administration:	Lisa (Pea) Saunders
Additional inspections:	Olwen Venn, Helen Allcorn, Robert and Lorely Forrester
Accounts:	Sheila Clifton, Maureen Humphries
Cover illustration:	David Sorrell
Cover design:	Caroline King
Symbols:	Celia Witchard, Emma Scragg and Lisa Saunders
Constant support:	The whole team at Alastair Sawday's Tours has provided constant support: Annie Shillito, Dave Kelly and Eliza Meredith.

There really IS a magic about Ireland; our experience over the last year tells us so.

We knew that the houses were interesting, and, in many cases, ravishingly lovely; we knew, too, that among the owners were some remarkable people. But quite how remarkable we were not aware! Of all the folk with whom we deal, in 5 countries, the Irish owners and hotel-keepers are the most easy-going and appreciative. And, needless to say, they seem to have the richest sense of humour.

We have had some hilarious letters from amused and happy readers, describing encounters in these Irish homes and hotels that could happen nowhere else. So if you dare to believe that there is still life in the old adages about Ireland, then go and see for yourself.

The EEC may finally cajole us all into eating the same sausages and taking the same medicines but Ireland gives us hope that the bureaucrats may yet fail to squeeze us all into the same mould. Even the foreigners who have taken root there - and there are many in this book - have absorbed the local passion for the moment, that delight in the absurdities and small idiosyncracies of every day. There are Japanese, Dutch, German, English, French within these pages, usually with an Irish spouse; but they all seem to be as alive to life as their hosts.

Whatever you plan to do in Ireland - be it touring, sailing, cycling or just staying put - I urge you to peer over the hedges and make friends with the help of this extraordinary book. And as an added bonus you may also eat delicious food and see hidden places of ineffable beauty.

Alastair Sawday

INTRODUCTION

We were thrilled that the first edition of this book sold out so quickly and with such positive feedback. Readers kindly wrote in to tell us about their trips to Ireland using Special Places as their bible. Nearly always this was to say that the book had faithfully done its job.

However, an owner may have a bad day; a series of things will go wrong on one occasion, leaving an unfavourable impression - we can't account for all of the people all of the time. But where a place has not lived up to expectations for serious reasons they have been removed. This usually means dirty, cold, damp, or unfriendly. This is of crucial importance to us and I thank all of you who brought reasonable gripes to my attention.

This year it is the best of the first edition who remain, and there are some fifty engaging new places to replace less successful entries. The test of time is a vital component in building the perfect book.

I have visited every entry (bar two). The variety is rich and extraordinary. There are lighthouses, mills, castles, Georgian homes, converted dairies, fishing lodges, thatched cottages, country house hotels, restaurants with rooms, townhouses, farms, old rectories and manses, a converted workhouse, small hotels, and even a converted church.

The price range, too, is wide and the spread even.

£15 - £20: 32 places
£20 - £25: 53 places
£25 - £40: 56 places
£40 - £70: 50 places

You really can choose your price in every county. Luxury, of course, varies with price... but people don't. I recommend this selection to you without reservation.

One last point about money: every owner pays a small fee to be included in this book. But it is a fee, not a bribe! We stand firmly by the integrity of all our 'Special Places' books. Once we include the wrong people for the wrong reasons we will cease to be 'special'.

IRELAND AS DESTINATION

Where nearly every other western European country has been picked over with microscope and tweezers for its every last ounce of original culture, its last square foot of pristine beach and its last inhabitant genuinely pleased to meet a tourist, Ireland remains refreshingly itself. If you are travelling across from Britain, Ireland can seem like a romantic vision of the past, a forgotten way of life, a time when people stopped and talked to each other in shops, when car traffic was thinly spread, when hold-ups occurred because of farmers moving livestock, when pubs were places of conversation, music, even dancing rather than pinball, quiz machines and Sky Sports... The Irish are great conversationalists, using a wide vocabulary and a constantly surprising and delightful turn of phrase. Any new face with a strange accent inspires friendly curiosity rather than jingoistic *froideur*. Courtesy, humour, curiosity and hospitality underpin the Irish character. However, the economic boom is changing the traditional face of Ireland fast. Good news for a lagging economy and its people but not for the independent traveller. There are ways of getting the most out of a visit to Ireland under Holidays in Ireland and Time to Visit.

GEOGRAPHY

In Ireland wonderful ruined abbeys sit in fields for all to explore. Rarely are its treasures bound up with fences and kiosks and 'this way' signs. The ruins of castles, priories, old manor houses, farm buildings and round towers litter the countryside and are one of the most resonant images of Ireland. Ivy, not the shamrock, should be its national emblem. The countryside is what Ireland is all about. Apart from perhaps Dublin, Belfast, Londonderry, Cork, Galway and Waterford Irish towns begin and end very suddenly. None of the straggling industrial estates, none of the roundabouts and ring roads that besiege large rural towns in Britain. The population of Ireland is only 4.5 million. Here you drive down the main drag with its brightly-coloured shop fronts and out into uninterrupted green fields and small lanes. There is great variety: forested hills (Wicklow and Antrim); barren mountains (Connemara and Donegal); fjord-like sea inlets (West Cork); strange and majestic rock formations (The Burren in Clare, the Giant's Causeway in Antrim, the Cliffs of Moher in Clare); lakelands (Fermanagh, Westmeath, Connemara, Leitrim, Sligo, Longford); rivers and restored heritage gardens; there are lovely beaches in Waterford, Wexford, Cork, Donegal, Sligo, Mayo; and megalithic tombs, barrows, dolmens and cairns crown the hilltops everywhere. Really the quantity of historical sites in Ireland is quite bewildering. There is not a county in Ireland, North or South, that I wouldn't recommend for one reason or another. Ireland is a paradise for walkers, archaeology enthusiasts, fishermen... but mainly it is the quality of human contact that lingers in the mind most vividly.

ROADS

There are very few dual carriageways in the south. Roads tend to be accompanied by a narrower lane that is half hard shoulder, half lane for pulling over to let cars overtake. The general speed of life in Ireland is reflected in the patience shown by other drivers. The Irish are likely to stop and chat with acquaintances at junctions, holding up those behind. Nobody hoots their horn. It is also common, especially in rural areas (i.e. nearly everywhere), to acknowledge other drivers (or anyone standing beside the road) by raising the forefinger of the steering hand as you pass. Do make sure it's the forefinger. I found after a while that I had moved my normal hand position to the top of the wheel so my gesture of solidarity could be seen. I was worried people would see my number plate and think the British unfriendly. This, of course, does not apply on major roads or (extremely infrequent) motorways.

Another side-effect of the economic boom has been the essential but painful process of upgrading the infrastructure. This means that roads all over Ireland are being rebuilt. Combine this with a massive increase in car-ownership and the fact that the roads that do exist are often insufficient to cope, there are times when you will be surprised at how long it takes to get anywhere. Always leave lots of time and don't try to do too much. Settle in one place for a few days and go walking and meet the people. Those who zoom round ticking sites off a list have come to the wrong place.

Dublin is a nightmare for traffic

SIGN-POSTING

Most of Ireland is a bewildering cat's cradle of tiny lanes which, these days, may rollercoaster alarmingly at times, but are rarely pot-holed. I don't think many Irish would disagree with me when I say that sign-posting in Ireland is appalling. A typical scenario for the hapless motorist would be the following: see signpost marked "Ballydehob 4". If it's an old sign this will be miles. If new, kilometres. You follow the small road for 2 miles until another sign says "Ballydehob 6" down an even smaller lane. This is the one that arrives at a farm or merely peters out at a field or cliff. If you understandably suspect that the last sign was turned by exuberant revellers returning from a pub (a national sport I'm afraid) you will continue to the next T-junction where there will be no sign whatsoever. If you chance your arm on one of the roads in front of you, rather than sensibly returning whence you came, there is a good chance you'll never be seen again.

This is only a mild overstatement and, while charming in a way, it does mean that your hosts often have a lot of soothing to do with new arrivals. On one occasion in County Cork I followed big, confident-looking signs near Kinsale for 5 miles to a bridge over one of the myriad inlets of the region. When I got there I discovered that the bridge had been demolished and moved 4 miles upstream... some years ago.

The whole business of signposts is much discussed in Ireland.

THE IRISH AND DIRECTIONS.

You will probably have heard that the Irish people are famous for their inability quickly and concisely to give directions. This is amazingly true.

My advice is to buy a massive-scale ordnance survey map and be very careful. Or get to the nearest big town and ask in a garage for the name of the person you're looking for. It's a small population and people notice each other. They should know. And if they don't, then it will become a point of honour to find someone who does. You should be wary of postal addresses too. They often contain ancient townland names that are nothing more than fields. They don't appear on maps and I can't see the point in them. Anyway, good luck.

PETROL

Nearly all garages have attendants who will fill up for you - no tip required. Some garages are just two pumps outside the local post-office-cum-stationer's-cum-chartered accountant's-cum-abbattoir etc. And often there's a barrel of beer somewhere in a darkened corner too.

NORTHERN IRELAND

You will, no doubt, have followed the wonderful-looking peace process in the North over the last two years, culminating in the Good Friday agreement and the Nobel peace prize for John Hume and David Trimble: "The mountain of sectarianism is behind us now ... People should not be confused by its shadow". For the moment we hold our breath, but this time it looks real.

The atmosphere in the North has radically changed over the last year. There is a tangible spirit of optimism in the air. Bars and restaurants are opening everywhere. And visitors are beginning to return to the province's natural treasures: the Mountains of Mourne in County Down, the Glens of Antrim, the Giant's Causeway, the Fermanagh lakes and the historic towns and cities of Belfast, Londonderry and Armagh.

Now is a good time to go.

By the way Londonderry and Derry are the same place, sometimes known as 'Stroke City'.

HOLIDAYS IN IRELAND

The most common mistake when planning a trip to Ireland is to assume that distances there carry the same time allowances as in other countries. I met many a weary couple who'd tried to 'do' Connemara, Cork, Dublin, the Burren and the Kerry peninsulas in 5 days. On the map it looks an hour's drive in the morning and a full day's sightseeing. In fact it's a full day's driving, which is to miss the point of Ireland. If you've only got a week, get somewhere and stay for three days or more. If you don't slow down to the pace of life (and the pace of the roads!) you're in for a frustrating time.

I cannot emphasise this point strongly enough!

TIME OF YEAR

A lot of you can only get away in summer because of work and school-holiday pressures, but Ireland becomes very popular in the summer months. The peninsulas in Kerry for example are ringed Christo-like by an unbroken chain of tour buses in July and August. They all go round the Ring of Kerry anti-clockwise, Killarney to Kenmare, and I advise you to do the same. But visit Cork, Kerry and Connemara in the so-called shoulder seasons, or out of season and you'll have the place practically to yourself. In my view the best months to be in these areas are March, April, May, September and October. In mid-summer I would recommend those counties that have not been given so much air space by the Irish tourist board - the Midlands, for example, where the people are so friendly, the landscape so green. There was a policy of pushing the 'poor west' to build up tourism there and the rest of Ireland has remained relatively unknown. This is a perfect state of affairs for those with a more adventurous nature.

HOW TO USE THIS BOOK

Prices   All the prices in the book are per person sharing a room i.e. £35 p.p. means that a couple taking a double room would pay £70. This is inclusive of VAT and service except where stated. 'Sing. supp.' is short for single supplement and applies to single travellers taking a double room on their own. Clearly owners lose out unless they charge a little more. Often this is only enforced during the high season (May, June, July, August) when demand is greatest. Check ahead.

Alcohol   In Ireland you need different licences for different types of alcohol: beer, wines, spirits. Ask if you need to bring your own (BYO).

Telephone numbers   All the numbers in this book are local only. If you are calling from Britain to the Republic the code is: 00-353, then drop the 0. So, 026-47154 becomes 00353-26-47154. Northern Ireland is, of course, part of Britain and so requires no international code. Just ring the number printed. To ring Britain from The Republic of Ireland the code is: 00-44, then drop the 0. To call Northern Ireland from the Republic dial 08 and then the Northern Ireland number in full, not dropping the 0. From the United States to the South dial 011353 then the area code without the 0. For Northern Ireland and mainland Britain dial 01144 followed by the area code without the 0.

Pets   Although there is a symbol that tells you whether an establishment welcomes pets into the house or not, it is still worth ringing and checking. Owners, who are great pet lovers themselves may be reluctant on behalf of their other guests.

Maps and how to find places in a particular area   Our maps are thoroughly up-to-date but are for flagging the position of establishments only. You could get very lost indeed using them as road maps! (see Driving section of Introduction). Take a good detailed road map with you. If you know where you are going, turn to our general map to check the number of the relevant area map. Then turn to that map to find the places numbered in your area. Finally turn to those numbers and read the descriptions and make your choice. There are also two indexes at the back listing the surnames and place names in alphabetical order.

The Nature of B&B in Ireland   The one thing that most upsets B&B owners is being treated like a hotel! These are people's homes and they want to treat their guests as friends; they hope you will do likewise, with sensitivity, kindness... and punctuality (within reason). The second worst aspect of running a B&B is waiting up late for guests who were supposed to turn up at, say, 6.30. As the owner you don't know if they have had an accident, got held up for perfectly valid reasons... or just decided to cancel without bothering to ring. I do implore you to let your hosts know as early as possible if you have a change of plan, or if you are going to be late.

Money   It surprises some people to learn that the Republic of Ireland has its own currency, the punt, now cut adrift from the British pound and floating up and down in value against it. At the time of writing there is a 10% difference in value. Northern Ireland uses British pounds, but each bank there produces its own very different notes. If you're crossing the border several times and using cash-point machines at different banks it can be very confusing. Border counties often accept either, although it is polite to pay in the correct currency, or at least ask before paying. Prices in the book are in punts in the south, pounds in the north.

1999 also sees the introduction of the new improved Euro currency which is being adopted by The Republic but not Britain and therefore not Northern Ireland. Both currencies will be used while the Euro is being integrated. There is now a fixed rate of exchange between the punt and the Euro since January 1st 1999: 0.787564 Punts to one Euro to be exact. This is written in stone. The Euro will be confined to electronic business payments in the main and will probably not have any effect for the time being on paying for B&Bs and the like. The Punt will be discontinued in 2002 over a period of six months.

Restaurants   Food in Ireland is now fantastic. Ten years ago it wasn't.

Breakfast   They do this properly. You can expect a full Irish fry nearly everywhere, done to a high standard with good sausages and bacon, and a choice of eggs. Many places offer something out of the ordinary such as smoked salmon, kedgeree, mackerel, potato cakes. A full Irish breakfast differs from the English version in only a couple of ways: typically it should include white and black pudding and soda bread. In practically every case in this book the quality, variety and quantity of your breakfast should astonish you and set you up for the day.

Some Ideas for Enjoying the Culture of Ireland

* Attend an intercounty hurling championship match during the season - May to September. Savour the atmosphere in advance where rival fans share the same pubs and later on the same terraces. This is a very fast and skilful sport.
* Tune in to local radio stations - you'll get all the local news. Also Radio na Gaeltachta if you want to experience the language.
* Check your local area to see if there is a performance of Irish music and dancing organised by Comhaltas Ceoltoir' *f*ireann. It will be genuine, not staged for the tourist.
* Always take local advice on routes, scenery etc from your hosts. They know their area well.

Explanation of symbols

Treat each one as a guide rather than a concrete indicator. A few notes:

Working farm.

Children are positively welcomed but cots are not necessarily available. The text will give restrictions where relevant.

Pets are welcome to sleep in the house as long as they are properly trained.

Vegetarians catered for with advance warning.

indicates basic ground floor access and at least one accessible bedroom, but not full facilities for handicapped guests.

indicates full and approved wheelchair facilities for ground floor and at least one bedroom.

Swimming is possible on the premises or nearby in a pool, a lake, a river, or the sea.

No smoking anywhere in the house.

Riding facilities either on the property or owners prepared to organise riding within a five mile radius.

Owners have their own pets.

Only cash or cheques accepted (i.e no credit or debit cards).

You organise fishing, either on the premises or nearby.

DISCLAIMER

We make no claims to pure objectivity in judging our special places to stay. They are here because we like them. Our opinions and tastes are ours alone and this book is a statement of them; we cross our fingers and hope that you will share them.

We have done our utmost to get our facts right but apologise unreservedly for any mistakes that may have crept in. Sometimes, too, prices shift, usually upward, and 'things' change. We would be grateful to be told of any errors or changes, however small.

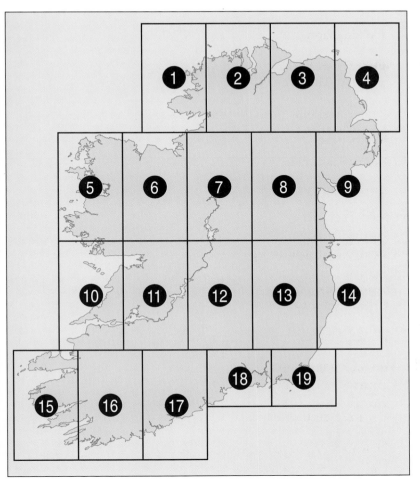

Ireland General Map

CONTENTS

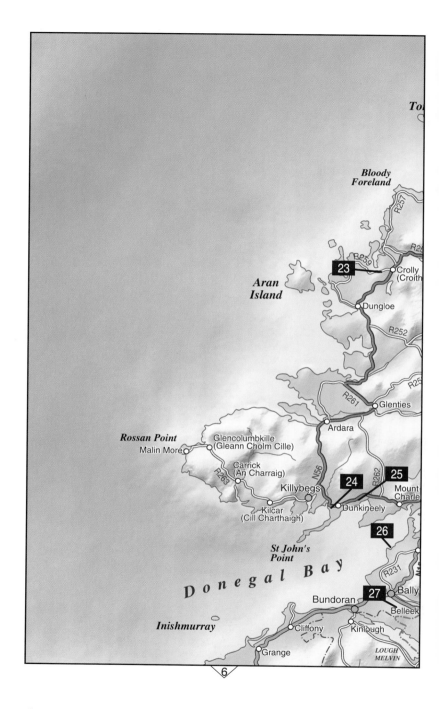

1   Map scale: 10 miles to 1 inch

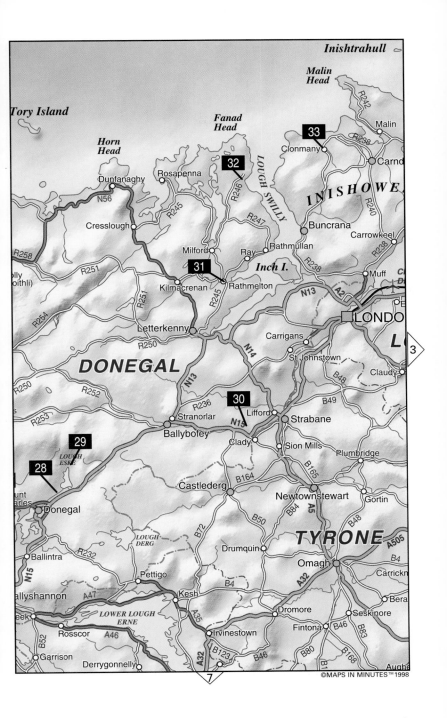

Tory Island

Inishtrahull

Malin
Head

Horn
Head

Fanad
Head

R242

33

Clonmany

R238

Malin

Carnd

Dunfanaghy

Rosapenna

32

LOUGH SWILLY

R240

INISHOWE

N56

R245

R246

R247

Cresslough

R251

Milford

Ray

Rathmullan

Buncrana

Carrowkeel

R238

R258

Inch I.

R238

Muff

oithli)

R251

31

Kilmacrenan

Rathmelton

N13

A2

Ce
D

R254

R245

Letterkenny

Carrigans

St Johnstown

LOND

L

LO

DONEGAL

N14

R250

Claudy

3

R250

R252

N13

R236

30

Lifford

B48

B49

Strabane

R253

Stranorlar

N15

Clady

Sion Mills

Plumbridge

29

Ballybofey

B165

LOUGH
ESKE

28

Castlederg

B164

Newtownstewart

Gortin

unt
arles

Donegal

B72

B50

B84

A5

B48

Ballintra

R232

LOUGH
DERG

Drumquin

TYRONE

A505

N15

Pettigo

Omagh

B4

Carrickn

allyshannon

A47

Kesh

B4

A32

Dromore

Bera

Rosscor

LOWER LOUGH
ERNE

A35

Fintona

Seskinore

eek

A46

Irvinestown

B46

B46

B83

Garrison

B52

Derrygonnelly

A32

B123

B46

B80

B168

Aughe

7

©MAPS IN MINUTES™ 1998

2

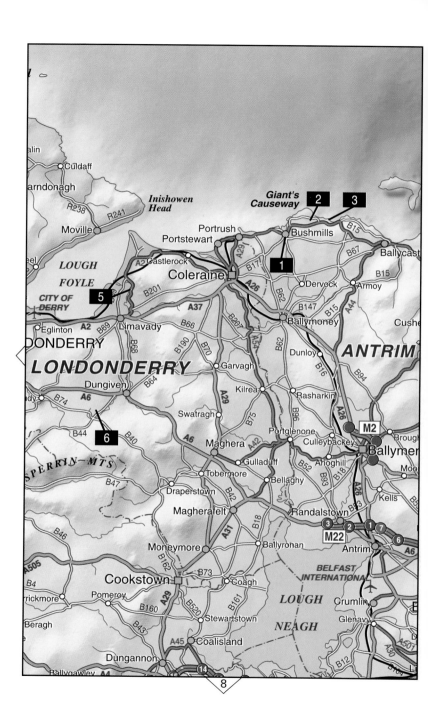

3

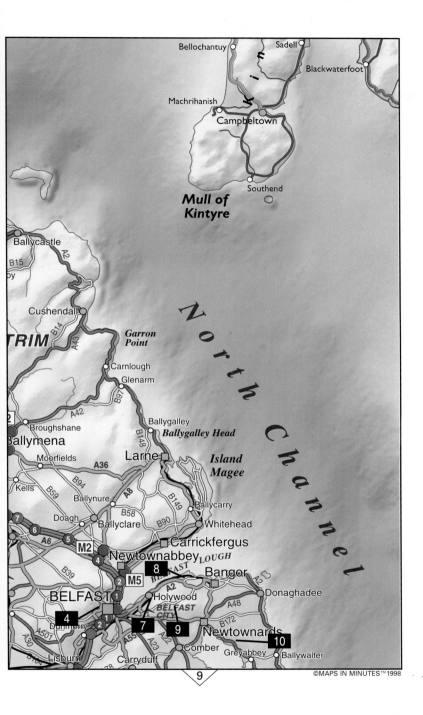

Bellochantuy
Sadell
Blackwaterfoot
Machrihanish
Campbeltown
Southend

Mull of Kintyre

Ballycastle
B15
A2
Cushendall
B14
TRIM
A43
Garron Point
Carnlough
Glenarm
B97
A42
Broughshane
Ballygalley
B148
Ballygalley Head
Ballymena
Moorfields
Larne
Island Magee
A36
Kells
B94
A8
B59
Ballynure
B149
Doagh
B58
Ballycarry
7
B90
Whitehead
6
Ballyclare
A6
5
M2
Carrickfergus
4
Newtownabbey *LOUGH*
B39
8
BELFAST
Bangor
2
M5
A2
BELFAST
1
Holywood
Donaghadee
4
BELFAST CITY
A48
2
B172
Dunmurry
7
9
Newtownards
A507
A55
A23
10
Lisburn
Carryduff
Comber
Greyabbey
Ballywalter

N o r t h   C h a n n e l

©MAPS IN MINUTES™ 1998

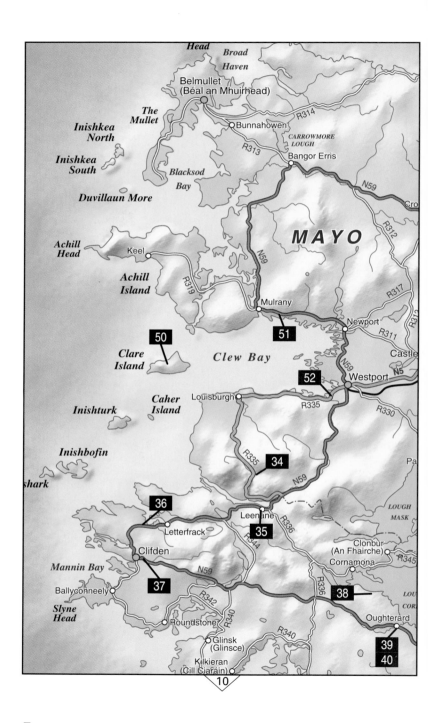

Head

Broad
Haven

Belmullet
(Béal an Mhuirhead)

The
Mullet

Inishkea
North

Bunnahowen

R314

CARROWMORE
LOUGH

R313

Inishkea
South

Bangor Erris

Blacksod
Bay

N59

Duvillaun More

Cro

R312

Achill
Head

Keel

MAYO

R317

Achill
Island

R319

R31

Mulrany

Newport

51

R311

Castle

Clare
Island

50

Clew Bay

N59

52

Westport

N5

Caher
Island

Louisburgh

Inishturk

R335

R330

Inishbofin

R335

34

N59

shark

LOUGH
MASK

36

Leenane

Letterfrack

Clonbur
(An Fhairche)

R345

Clifden

35

R344

Cornamona

Mannin Bay

N59

R336

38

LOU
COR

Ballyconneely

37

R342

R336

Oughterard

Slyne
Head

Roundstone

R340

R340

39

Glinsk
(Glinsce)

R340

40

Kilkieran
(Cill Chiaráin)

10

5

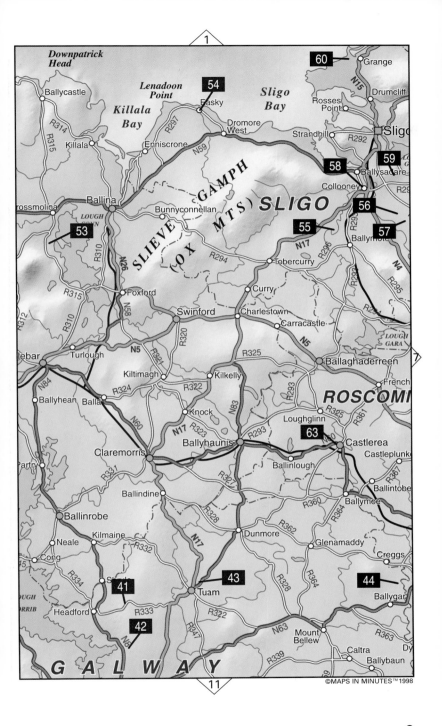

Downpatrick
Head

Ballycastle

Lenadoon
Point

60 Grange

54 Easky

Killala
Bay

Sligo
Bay

Rosses
Point

Drumcliff

R314

R315

Killala

Enniscrone

Dromore
West

Strandhill

Sligo

N59

R292

R297

58

59

Ballysadare

rossmolina

Ballina

Bunnyconnellan

Colloony

GAMPH

SLIGO

56

LOUGH
CONN

53

MTS)

55

57

SLIEVE

R310

R294

Tobercurry

N17

R296

Ballymote

N26

(O X)

Curry

R295

R315

Foxford

Charlestown

R294

Swinford

Carracastle

LOUGH
GARA

R312

R310

N58

R320

N5

lebar

Turlough

N5

R321

R325

Ballaghaderreen

French

N84

Kiltimagh

R324

R322

Kilkelly

R293

ROSCOM

Ballyhean

Balla

Knock

N83

R325

R361

Claremorris

N60

N17

R323

Ballyhaunis

R293

Loughglinn

63

Castlerea

Castleplunk

Partry

R331

Ballinlough

R367

Ballindine

R327

R360

Ballintobe

Ballinrobe

R328

Ballymoe

R364

Neale

Kilmaine

R362

Glenamaddy

R332

N17

Dunmore

R360

Creggs

Cong

R334

Sli

41

43

R328

R364

44

LOUGH
ORRIB

Headford

Tuam

Ballygar

42

R333

R322

R347

N63

Mount
Bellew

R363

R339

Caltra

Dy

G A L W A Y

Ballybaun

11

©MAPS IN MINUTES™ 1998

6

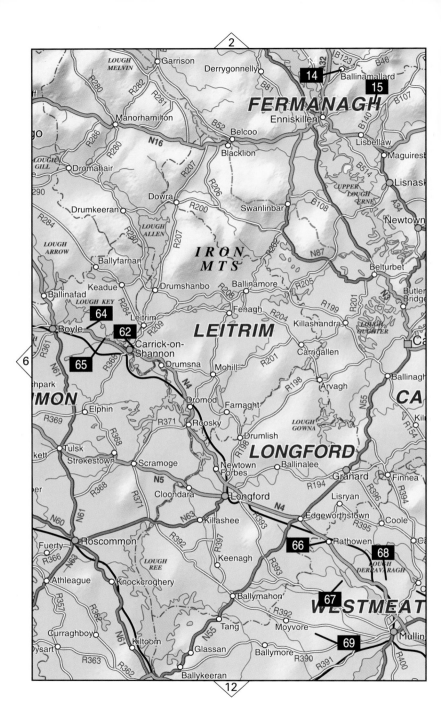

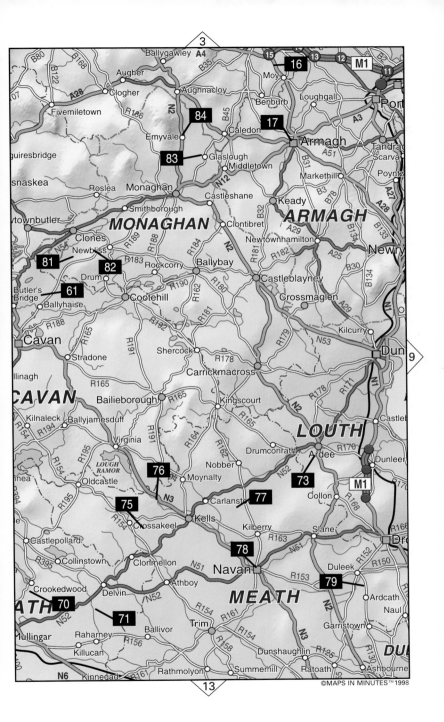

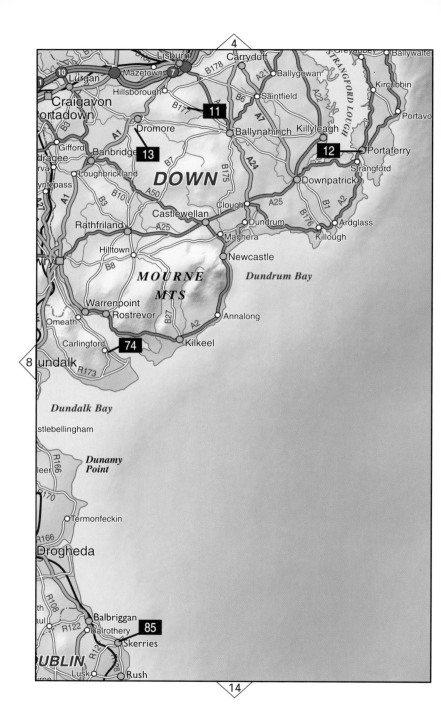

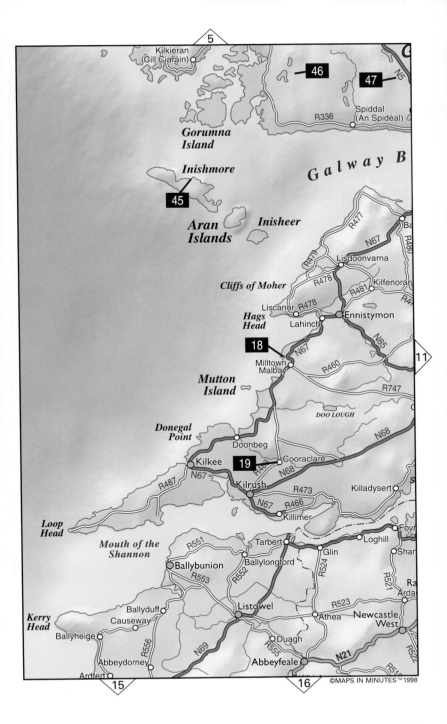

Kilkieran
(Cill Ciaráin)

46

47

N5

R336

Spiddal
(An Spidéal)

*Gorumna
Island*

G a l w a y B

Inishmore

45

R477

N67

R480

Ba

R479

Lisdoonvarna

*Aran
Islands*

Inisheer

R478

R481

Kilfenora

R4

Cliffs of Moher

R478

Liscanor

R478

*Hags
Head*

Lahinch

Ennistymon

18

N67

N85

11

Milltown
Malbay

R460

R747

*Mutton
Island*

DOO LOUGH

N68

*Donegal
Point*

Doonbeg

Kilkee

19

Cooraclare

N68

R487

N67

Kilrush

N67

R473

Killadysert

S

R466

Killimer

*Loop
Head*

*Mouth of the
Shannon*

R551

Tarbert

Loghill

Foy

Glin

Shar

R524

Ballybunion

R553

Ballylongford

R552

R521

Ra

Ard

*Kerry
Head*

Ballyduff

Listowel

R523

Athea

Newcastle
West

Causeway

Duagh

Ballyheige

R556

N69

R555

R5

R5

Abbeydorney

Abbeyfeale

N21

Ardfert

©MAPS IN MINUTES™ 1998

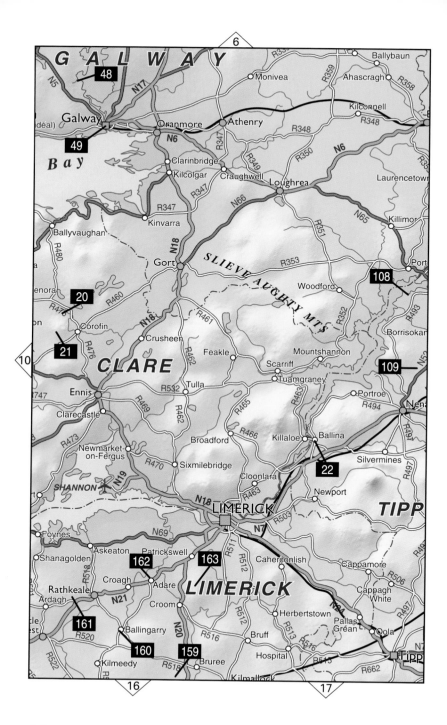

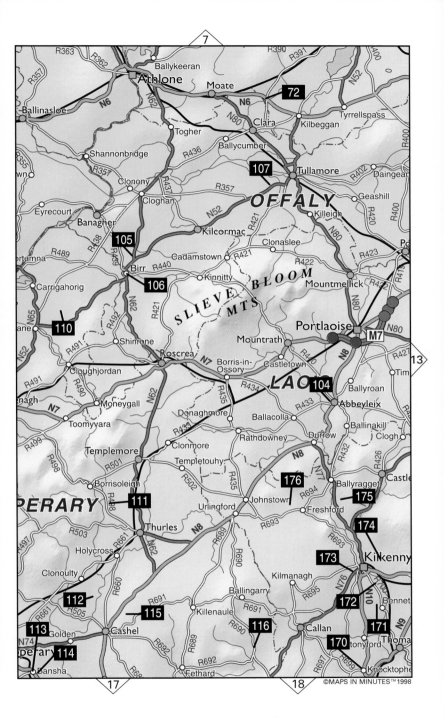

©MAPS IN MINUTES™ 1998

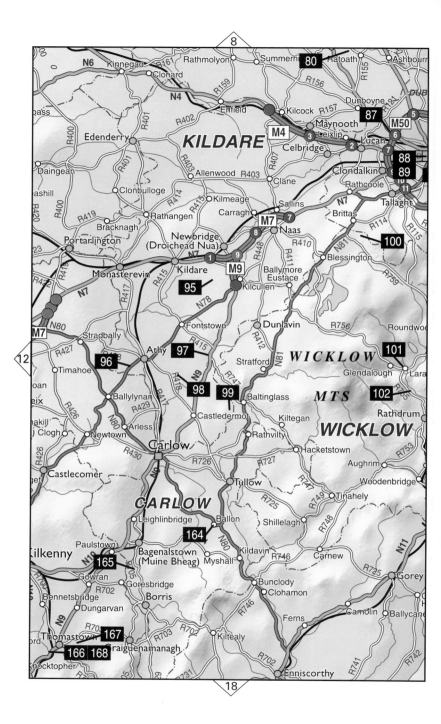

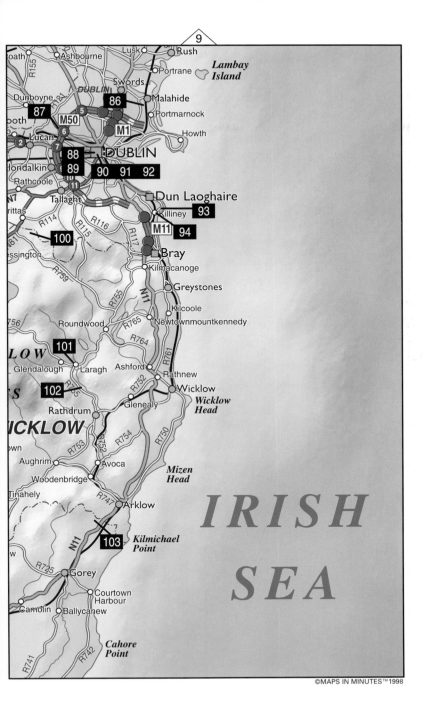

©MAPS IN MINUTES™1998

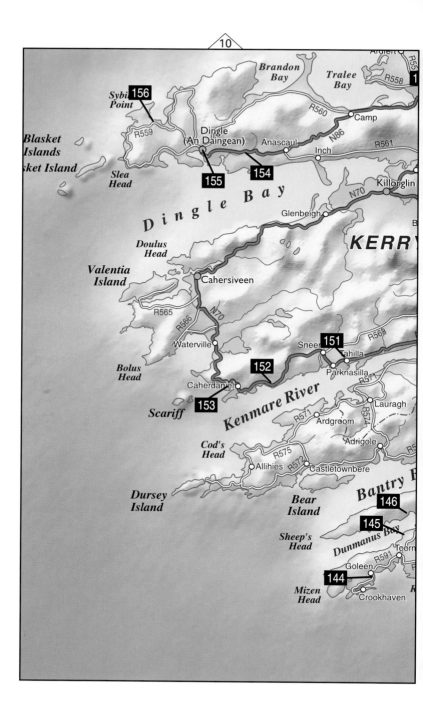

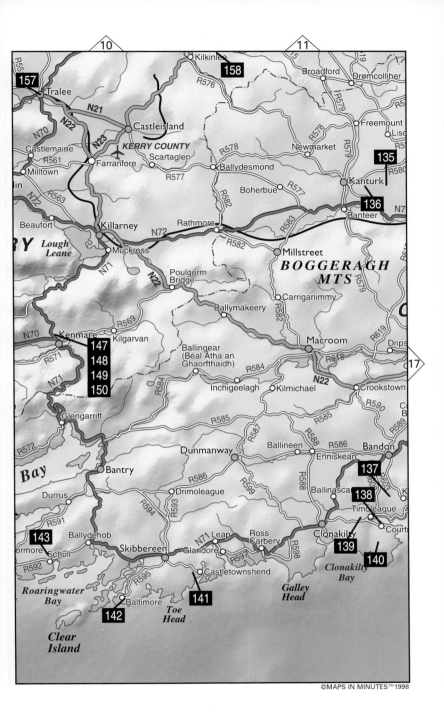

R55
157
Tralee
N21
N22
N23
Castleisland
Kilkinlea
R576
158
Broadford
Dromcolliher
R579
R5
Freemount
Liso
R5

KERRY COUNTY
N70
Castlemaine
R561
Milltown
Farranfore
Scartaglen
Ballydesmond
R578
Newmarket
R579
135
R5
R580

lin
N72
R563
Killarney
N72
Rathmore
R577
Boherbue
R577
Kanturk
136
N7
Banteer

RY
Lough Leane
Muckross
N71
N72
R582
R583
R582
Millstreet

BOGGERAGH MTS
R579

N22
Poulgorm Bridge
Carriganimmy
R582

Ballymakeery

R569
Kenmare
Kilgarvan
147
148
149
150
N70
R571
N71
Ballingear
(Béal Átha an Ghaorfthaidh)
R584
R584
Inchigeelagh
Kilmichael
N22
Macroom
R618
R619
Drips
17
Crookstown

R585
R585
R590
C
B

Glengarriff
R572
Bay
R585
R587
Dunmanway
Ballineen
R588
R586
Enniskean
R589
Bandon
R603
137

Durrus
Bantry
R586
R599
Drimoleague
R593
R594
R588
Ballinascarthy
138
Timoleague
Court

R591
Ballydehob
Skibbereen
N71
Leap
Glandore
R597
Ross Carbery
R598
Clonakilty
139
140

143
ormore
Schull
R592
Castletownshend
141
Galley Head
Clonakilty Bay

Roaringwater Bay
Baltimore
Toe Head
142

Clear Island

16

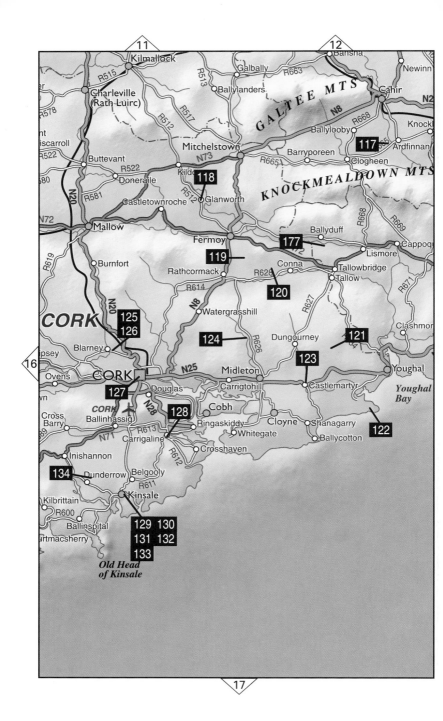

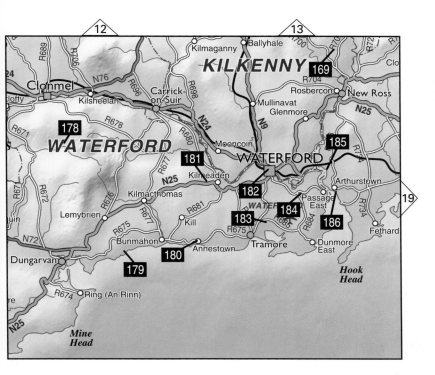

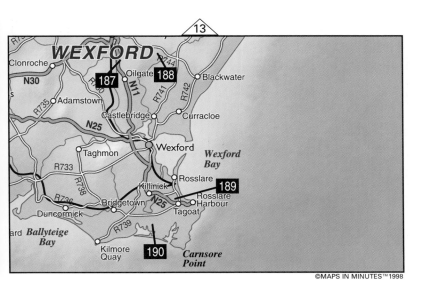

Antrim
•
Londonderry
•
Down
•
Fermanagh
•
Tyrone
•
Armagh
•

Northern Ireland

The Bushmills Inn

25 Main St
Bushmills
Co. Antrim
BT57 8QA

Tel: 012657-32339
Fax: 012657-32048
E-mail: info@bushmills~inn.com
www: http://www.bushmills-inn.com/

Roy Bolton and Richard Wilson

The Bushmills Inn goes way back to the time when the Giants' Causeway was first being formed... well almost. The oldest part of this former coaching inn is probably early 17th-century and every extension since has been added with an eye for the look of the whole. There is a round tower by the main entrance, a grand staircase, a circular library with a secret room, a turf fire that greets all-comers by the reception desk. Whitewashed walls, oil and gas lamps, flagstones, the open fire in the kitchen that links the bar to the hotel and pitched pine walls — they all set the tone here. Up the grand staircase there is a permanent gallery of James McKendry's oils and watercolours of the Causeway coastline. In the Coaching Inn the cottage style bedrooms are all different while, on the banks of the River Bush, the spacious Mill House rooms have their own sitting area and small dressing room. Naturally all rooms have standard mod cons such as phone and TV and such details as baby-listening facilities have not been overlooked! Everything from food to staff at the Bushmills is done to a T. There's not much to compare with it at this level.

Rooms: 32: Mill House: 1 suite, 19 tw/d, 2 fam. Coaching Inn: 4 sing, 4 d, 1 tw, 1 fam; all rooms en/s bath or sh.
Price: £44 — £59 p.p. Single room rate: £58. Single occupancy twin or double: £68 — £98.
Breakfast: Included — full Irish.
Meals: Restaurant dinners £22. Lunches and snacks à la carte.
Closed: Never!

How to get there: On the A4, Antrim coast road. From Ballymoney take the B62 turning right onto the B17 from Coleraine. Follow the Giants' Causeway signs.

Map Ref No: 3

Craig Park

24 Carnbore Rd
Bushmills
Co. Antrim
BT57 8YF

Tel: 012657-32496
Fax: 012657-32479
E-mail: craig.park@dial.pipex.com
www: web:http://ds.dial.pipex.com/craig.park/

Jan Cheal

Perfectly located for Northern Ireland's most famous tourist attraction, the amazing stone-columned steps of the Giant's Causeway, Craig Park sits on high ground with sweeping views that take in the Donegal Mountains. You can even see the Scottish islands of Jura and Islay on clear days. In 1995, Jan and David completed renovation of the original late 18th-century North Antrim farmhouse. They love having people of all nationalities sitting chatting around the table. It's a way for them to continue their extensive travels. They lived all over the world before settling here: two years in America, then Brazil, Puerto Rico and West Africa for seven years. Odds and ends they collected on the way grace the drawing room today, with African heads lining a window ledge. There is plenty of space and light throughout. Mahogany bannisters lead up to a landing. Here, double doors give onto a balcony and all the rooms are spotless and warm with rugs on the floor and nice wooden beds. You will be well looked after here by a very gregarious couple who put great emphasis on their high standards.

Rooms: 3: 2 twins and 1 family: all with en suite shower. There is also a separate bathroom.
Price: From £25 p.p. Sing. supp. £5.
Breakfast: Included — full Irish.
Meals: They recommend the Bushmills Inn and Sweeneys pub.
Closed: Christmas and New Year.

How to get there: From Bushmills follow signs to distillery. Immediately first left after distillery, then first right after Citroën garage, 1 mile then left onto Carnbore Rd. House signed to left.

Map Ref No: 3

Whitepark House

Whitepark Bay
Ballintoy
Co. Antrim
BT54 6NH

Tel: 012657-31482

Bob and Siobhán Isles

Walk the eight miles along stunning coastal cliffs from the Giant's Causeway until you reach Whitepark House, sitting up on high ground looking out to sea. On clear days you can see Rathlin lighthouse, Islay and the Paps of Jura. Bob will drive you one way so you can walk back. The house was built in 1735 and extended at the turn of the century and the feeling inside is extraordinary. Bob and Siobhán clearly love the business of entertaining and are keen for their guests not just to relax but also to experience all that this special area of Northern Ireland has to offer. So inside: wood beams, log fires, a lovely bay window in an open-plan hall where breakfast is taken, big double rooms which look over mock crenellations out to sea. But it is the quantity of greenery which colours and refreshes the house and which catches the eye first, particularly in the long drawing room: dried flowers, cactuses, baskets of green plants of all sizes, ferns... it's a greenhouse you can live in. At the back is a colourful flower-garden and a stream in a small dell. Breakfast was unimpeachable too.

Rooms: 3: 2 doubles and 1 twin: all sharing 1 bathroom and 1 extra loo.
Price: £22.50 p.p. Sing. supp. £3.50.
Breakfast: Included — full Irish.
Meals: Bob and Siobhán will recommend places to eat.
Closed: Never!

How to get there: From Bushmills take the coast road to Whitepark Bay (A2). Go past youth hostel entrance, 100 yds on right.

Map Ref No: 3

Greenwood House

25 Park Rd
Belfast
Co. Antrim
BT7 2FW

Tel: 01232-202525
Fax: 01232-202530
E-mail: greenwood.house@virgin.net

Jason and Mary Harris

This late Victorian redbrick house has been done up by Jason and Mary with great brio and individuality and the result is very bright, cheerful, contemporary, different. Maple wood floors with pastel yellow and blue walls, stripey modern furniture and some lovely, thin, Giacometti-like, wrought-iron chairs; wooden tables and dresser, very bright yellow and red curtains, high ceilings, big windows, lots of light. As you climb the stairs there are things to notice all around: brightly-coloured crêpe-paper lamp shades, modern pictures by Ulster artists, a Big Sleep poster. (Jason looked a bit sheepish about that one!) The bedrooms are no less interesting; the wrought-iron motif is continued, as are the bright colours, while bathrooms are very white and have properly deep baths you can lie in. Top quality breakfasts and extremely comfortable beds complete the tableau. Greenwood House is a homely, warm place looking straight onto Ormeau Park and golf course... and Jason and Mary are fun and easy-going. *Special Places guests should reveal themselves, as Jason will give you the best rooms.*

Rooms: 7: 1 single, 1 family, 2 twins and 3 doubles; 3 with en suite bath and shower; 4 with en suite shower.
Price: £25 p.p. Sing. supp. £10.
Breakfast: Included — full Irish.
Meals: Excellent choice locally.
Closed: Christmas week and New Year.

How to get there: From city centre follow signs to Newcastle/Downpatrick up the A24 Ormeau Rd, over bridge, 500 yards up turn left. House on right.

Map Ref No: 4

Streeve Hill

25 Dowland Road
Limavady
Co. Londonderry
BT49 0HP

Tel: 015047-66563
Fax: 015047-68285

Peter and June Welsh

On the outskirts of Drenagh estate lies this 1730s farmhouse, a dower house to Drenagh House. When Peter and June Welsh decided to move from Drenagh there was work to be done... such as replacing the top storey with weathered red brick. The result today is a large but manageable home with informal and comfortable rooms. This is a place for log fires, long chatty dinners over excellent food with ingredients always in season, coffee in deep sofas. A menu example: Ballycastle lobster cocktail; fillet of beef, new potatoes, fresh garden spinach, Béarnaise sauce; Irish cheeses; strawberry and elderflower 'bombe'... all local, all fresh, all delicious. During the day you can visit the lovely Drenagh gardens for a nominal £2.50 or sit out with a book in the sheltered south-west facing courtyard and walled garden. Your bedrooms are bright and cheerful, with brass beds and antique furniture and charming views of the surrounding parkland. There will be proper linen on the beds and great attention to detail. Peter and June are charming hosts and treat their visitors as personal guests.

Rooms: 3: 2 doubles with baths en suite; 1 twin with en suite shower.
Price: £45 p.p. Sing. supp. £5. 10-15% discounts for longer stays.
Breakfast: Included — full Irish.
Meals: Dinner £30 with 24 hours advance notice. Packed lunches on request £5.
Closed: December 16th — January 5th.

How to get there: From Limavady take B201 for Castlerock, follow Drenagh estate wall on right. 200 yards past lodge turn right at end of wall, up lane to first big house.

Map Ref No: 3

Drumcovitt House

704 Feeny Rd
Feeny
Co. Londonderry
BT47 4SU

Tel: 015047-81224
Fax: 015047-81224
E-mail: drumcovitt.feeny@btinternet.com
www: http://drumcovitt.farm-holidays.com

Florence Sloan

Driving along small roads out from Londonderry I spied an intriguing old farmhouse on a hill, saluted by a lovely weeping ash to the front. Florence dealt with me as I'm sure she deals with everyone — she is calm, friendly and down-to-earth. The house is Irish Georgian (1796) and has many interesting features such as original windows with small lower panes, a huge door in the hall with wooden drop bar that would stop the most determined burglar in his tracks. Grand rooms downstairs have round bays, original pine flooring, gilt pelmets, ancient carpets, dado rails, cornices... the full Georgian Monty. Take the stairs up to a wide, creaky, arched landing off which lie large bedrooms with great views across fields and mature beeches to the Sperrin Mountains — people hang-glide from the highest spur. On a misty morning these peaks and the spire of Banagher church are all you can see. Walk up to the old church and climb the glen to the reservoir and filter house, or take the back lane from the house to woodland, a ring fort, bogland. Exceptional value.

Rooms: 3: 2 twins and 1 family sharing 1 bathroom and shower and 1 shower-room.
Price: £18 — £20 p.p. No sing. supp.
Breakfast: Included — full Irish.
Meals: Dinner à la carte from £5 — £17 (book before midday). Packed lunches about £3.
Closed: Never!

How to get there: From Derry follow signs to Belfast (A6) for 7 miles, turn right towards Feeny/Claudy on B74 for 5 miles. Through Feeny, 0.5 miles, house on left.

Map Ref No: 3

Carnwood House

85 Victoria Rd
Holywood
Co. Down
BT18 9BG

Tel: 01232-421745
Fax: 01232-421745

Jenny Foster

Buried in the trees in the lovely lough-side village of Holywood is this large square 1840s town residence. And Jenny's welcome is easy, open and friendly. You will be taken in hand, given tea and scones in one of the gigantic drawing rooms with its Persian carpets, marble fireplace, ornate plasterwork ceilings and long windows looking onto the garden. Here, guests eat excellent breakfasts all together. There are only three bedrooms upstairs, all equally generous in proportion, some with canopies and there's one four-poster; very comfortable and plush, with new windows which keep them warm and quiet. Not that this is a noisy corner of the world — that's one of its charms. You are on Belfast Lough and it's only a short drive into the city. But also you can stroll out for lovely walks in the Craigantlet Hills. Other popular pastimes are riding and fishing (within 10 minutes of the house) and paint effect courses which take place right across the way. This is a place to find a very personal welcome and enjoy both town and country in a peaceful, secluded, leafy setting.

Rooms: 3: all doubles with en suite shower.
Price: £30 p.p. Sing. supp. £5.
Breakfast: Included — full Irish.
Meals: Packed lunches £4.50. Lots of excellent restaurants in Holywood.
Closed: Never!

How to get there: From Belfast take A2 to Holywood. At Holywood sign on dual carriageway go on to third set of traffic lights, turn right and immediately left onto Croft Rd. After 250 yds first right into Victoria Rd. 50 yds on left up small lane.

Map Ref No: 4

Carrig-Gorm

27 Bridge Road
Helen's Bay, Bangor
Co. Down
BT19 1TS

Tel: 01247-853680

Roland and Elisabeth Eves

Elizabeth and Roland are an immensely friendly couple and this is immediately apparent. They're so concerned that you have everything you need that you almost feel you're doing *them* a favour by asking. Helen's Bay is a lovely, leafy, upmarket suburb of Belfast (eight miles) with big detached houses strung out, each in its own garden, with its own entrance drive. Carrig-gorm (late 18th/part Victorian) is one such. Downstairs there is stark contrast between the dark wood-panelled hall and the very bright, fully glassed conservatory with its wicker furniture where we took real coffee and chatted. Everything in the house is immaculate and there are some interesting pieces of antique furniture and ornaments. The drawing room has blue velvet seating, and a deep, thick carpet and there's a log fire for the winter in the lounge hall. The bedrooms are voluminous and warm, with proper bathrooms. There were a little vase of flowers, a basket of shampoos and a bowl of fruit in my room, and I slept like a log in the big bed.

Rooms: 3: 1 family with en suite bathroom; 1 twin and 1 single sharing bathroom.
Price: £23 — £28 p.p. Sing. supp. £5 — £8.
Breakfast: Included — full Irish.
Meals: Available nearby at the Old Inn in Crawfordsburn.
Closed: Christmas and New Year.

How to get there: From Belfast take A2 for 8 miles — turn left for Helen's Bay. 1 mile, then turn right into Bridge Rd — 4th house on left.

Map Ref No: 4

Beech Hill

23 Ballymoney Rd
Craigantlet, Holywood
Co. Down
BT23 4TG

Tel: 01232-425892
Fax: 01232-425892
E-mail: beech.hill@btinternet.com

Victoria Brann

It might surprise you that Beech Hill was only built thirty years ago as it has all the characteristics and atmosphere of a much older house. Victoria is full of energy and is a natural hostess. She and her two dogs — Mistle, a lurcher, and Swift, a whippet — will usher you into a long sitting room where the flowers and green and yellow colouring reminded me of a pond, and a lily-pad motif does indeed cover the green/blue sofa. Through the windows there are fields, cows, hills, and a croquet lawn. Delicious cakes and tea appear soon after you are settled. The whole house is on one floor. Go one way and you come to a wooden conservatory with wicker furniture and hanging baskets filled with geraniums. Go the other and you come to the bedrooms: decorated with plain pale colours, they are all immaculate, with comfortable beds, mod cons like TV and telephone, good quality linen and demure prints of Belfast on the walls. The house is a warm place and Victoria is chatty and friendly. It's always a relief to find you've arrived somewhere genuine.

Rooms: 3: 1 twin/king with en suite bath; 1 double with en suite bath & shower; 1 queen double with en/s shower.
Price: £30 p.p. Sing. supp. £5.
Breakfast: Included — full Irish.
Meals: Available nearby at The Old Inn and Shanks.
Closed: Never!

How to get there: From Belfast take A2 towards Bangor. Bypass Holywood. 1.5 miles from bridge at Ulster Folk Museum, turn right up Ballymoney Rd, signed to Craigantlet. House 1.75 miles on left.

Map Ref No: 4

Edenvale House

130 Portaferry Road
Newtownards
Co. Down
BT22 2AH

Tel: 01247-814881
Fax: 01247-826192

Diane and Gordon Whyte

Diane is one of those people everyone seems to know, like and talk about before you get there: incredibly friendly, bursting with energy and chat and never far from laughter. You approach Edenvale (1780 plus extensions) up a drive which starts right by the gently lapping waters of Strangford Lough. Two minutes drive down the coast is the National Trust property, Mountstewart, and a short ferry ride from Portaferry takes you to Castle Ward, also National Trust. Downstairs at Edenvale, meanwhile, there is a big kitchen that is obviously HQ for operations, a very bright sunroom whose doors look out over the lake and the Mourne Mountains, and a sitting room with marble fireplaces, gracefully devoid of TV. The bedrooms are large, well-proportioned, immaculate, and with beds — two of them huge — that have pelmets and hangings. A lot of effort goes into each aspect of the Edenvale experience, including the lovely big flower garden which is heavy-laden with roses. This is also a great place for kids.

Rooms: 3: 1 family and 1 double with en suite bath and shower; 1 twin with en suite shower.
Price: £27.50 p.p. Sing. supp. £5.
Breakfast: Included — full Irish.
Meals: Available in Bangor.
Closed: December 22nd — January 2nd.

How to get there: From Newtownards take A20 Portaferry Rd. Edenvale is only 2 miles outside Newtownards up a drive on the left.

Map Ref No: 4

Fortwilliam Country House

210 Ballynahinch Rd
Hillsborough
Co. Down
BT26 6BH

Tel: 01846-682255/683401
Fax: 01846-689608

Terry and Mavis Dunlop

Fortwilliam, a large, square-set house in tranquil hills, is in fact 300 years old: its bay-windowed front was only added in the 1930s. Inside, the decor is partly reminiscent of the '30s period with some very daring carpet colours, hunting prints on the walls, bubble glass here and there. Terry is a busy farmer with a large suckling herd to care for and two very friendly dogs. Mavis loves to chat at length over the fresh tea and home-made cakes that are always ready for visitors in her lovely country-style kitchen (warming Aga, baskets hanging from beams). Rooms are excellent: the garden room has a window seat onto a daisy-strewn lawn; there is some lovely furniture, too. Your bathroom may be pink and will have masses of soaps, sachets and squeezy bottles. There is always a log fire burning in the snug sitting room; or sit out in the little walled garden and enjoy the view of the hills. In short, you will be coddled, and the Dunlops deserved their 1996 Ulster Guesthouse of the Year award.

Rooms: 3: 1 double with en suite shower; 1 double with own bathroom; 1 double with own shower-room.
Price: £25 p.p. Sing. supp. £5.
Breakfast: Included — full Irish.
Meals: Good restaurant in Hillsborough.
Closed: Never!

How to get there: From Hillsborough take the Ballynahinch Rd for 3.5 miles — house up steep drive to right (on a hill).

Map Ref No: 9

The Narrows

8 Shore Rd
Portaferry
Co. Down
BT22 1JY

Tel: 012477-28148
Fax: 012477-28105
E-mail: the.narrows@dial.pipex.com
www: http://www.fjordlands.org/strngfrd/narrow1.h

Will and James Brown

The Narrows is new but it must become a well-loved institution before long.
Brothers Will and James have returned to the birthplace of their father to create a
stylish shore-front restaurant and guesthouse with a youthful, bright, modern-yet-
comfortable feel that is all its own. Reception and service are exceptionally friendly,
the informal restaurant abustle with its wooden tables and views across Strangford
Lough. Delicious seafood from both sea and lough is recommended; high quality
and good value rather than over-elaboration is the house style. I can vouch for the
mussels myself. Just as much effort has gone into the rooms which are well designed
and have lovely views of the lough. They are modernly furnished with low beds,
matting carpets, plain whites and creams on the walls, not too much decoration, the
overall effect successfully restful on the eye. There is colour too — in window-boxes
of flowers, in the paintings of local artists on the walls of the common areas. This is
an area of outstanding natural beauty and there is certainly no more friendly or
relaxing place from which to explore it.

Rooms: 13: all doubles or twins with en
suite bath or shower.
Price: £37 p.p. Sing supp. £8.
Breakfast: Included — full Irish.
Meals: Restaurant: Lunches and dinner à
la carte (main course average £10).
Closed: Never!

How to get there: From Belfast take A20
south to Portaferry (28 miles) — house on
shore front.

Map Ref No: 9

Sylvan Hill House
76 Kilntown Rd
Dromore
Co. Down
BT25 1HS

Tel: 01846-692321
Fax: 01846-692321

Elise Coburn

Elise and Jimmy enjoy the bustle of human presence that makes a house feel lived in so, when the kids had grown up, they started B&B. Guests almost always eat with Elise and Jimmy. She is a very good self-trained chef and offers wine with the meal without extra charge... within reason! Breakfasts are great too, with home-made bread and free-range eggs. The old house (1781) sits on a hill and from its vantage point you can see for miles over the Mourne and Dromara Mountains. In summer you can enjoy the view while dining in the plant-filled conservatory. Elise describes it as a one-and-a-half storey house because from the front it appears to have only one. It's actually a bigger house than it seems from the outside and Elise keeps it immaculate. The rooms remind one that children have been brought up here and comfortable beds sit on little platforms. There's a large en suite bathroom which also has a platform and the bath is kept company by mini-chairs and mirrors. This is a house with plenty of idiosyncrasy and your hosts are open and easy-going.

Rooms: 3: 2 doubles with en suite bathroom; 1 double/twin with own shower-room.
Price: £25 p.p. No sing. supp.
Breakfast: Included — full Irish.
Meals: Dinner £15 (3 courses including wine).
Closed: Never!

How to get there: From Belfast M1 towards Dublin, then Sprucefield Roundabout onto A1 towards Dublin. At the Hillsborough bypass take Donaghloney Rd to right. Exactly 4 miles turn left to Dromore. House 0.25 miles on left at top of hill.

Map Ref No: 9

13

Rossfad House

Killadeas
Ballinamallard
Co. Fermanagh
BT94 2LS

Tel: 01365-388505

John and Lois Williams

Rossfad is a Georgian house (1776) which lies in the heart of the Fermanagh lakelands. The main lakes are Upper and Lower Lough Erne with many subsidiary arterial rivers, smaller lakes, forest parks, castles. The Victorian guest wing, added in 1876, has its own access and south-facing guest rooms, all going on to long views of the garden, trees, then the lake, then the mountains. Beautiful in sunlight, magical in moonlight. A long avenue separates the house from the road, so only the sounds of nature and family life surround you. There is simple but comfortable furniture in the guest living room and, again, those views from windows on two sides. Big bedrooms are simply decorated and bathrooms have massive baths. While there's an open fire for chilly evenings, whatever sunlight there is floods into the sitting room over breakfast. This is a place for peace and contemplation, although croquet and badminton can be played in the garden, and there's swimming in the lake.

Rooms: 2: both doubles/triples: 1 with en suite bathroom; 1 with private bathroom.
Price: £17.50 p.p. Sing. supp. £2.50.
Breakfast: Included — full Irish.
Meals: Not available.
Closed: December — March.

How to get there: From Enniskillen take Kesh Rd for exactly 5 miles (A32 to Trory for 2 miles, then B82 for 3 miles). Avenue opposite road to Whitehill Rd — trees at the end of unsurfaced road up to house.

Tempo Manor

Tempo
Co. Fermanagh
BT94 3PA

Tel: 013655-41953
Fax: 013655-41202
E-mail: john@tempoweb.com
www: http://www.btinternet.com/~tempo.manor/

John and Sarah Langham

Tempo is breathtaking — a heady mix of museum-like nostalgia for times and Langhams past, an idyllic rural environment and a very bright, living, young household. Sarah has firmly put her artistic stamp on the place so that now bold colours vivify dark passages and below-ground-floor rooms. John created an amazing blue bathroom — the one with the wash stand and gold stars — in one weekend. As Sarah says, "John does all the carpentry, I do all the soft bits." And all the eccentricity sits well with the family portraits and ancient scrolls of Langhams who have been made archbishop in the 13th century and so forth. They have made absolutely sure, however, that comfort has not played second fiddle to artistic whimsy, in case you were worried: super-king-size-four-poster-beds, 6-foot baths, loads of hot water, thick bathrobes, electric blankets, new and best quality linen. The house sits by a perfect natural lake which almost laps the walls of the house. People come here just to be able to stay in such a place, but also for the fishing and shooting. One of the most special places to stay in all Ireland, north or south.

Rooms: 4: 1 four-poster with en suite bath; 2 twins and 1 four-poster with private bath.
Price: £50 p.p.
Breakfast: Included — full Irish.
Meals: Dinners for large parties by arrangement. Otherwise restaurants in Enniskillen — menus at Tempo.
Closed: End October — March 1st.

How to get there: From Enniskillen take B80 into Tempo. Past church, turn right at Spa supermarket signed Brookborough — 0.25 miles "private road" sign by gates on left.

Map Ref No: 7

Grange Lodge

Grange Rd
Dungannon
Co. Tyrone
BT71 7EJ

Tel: 01868-784212
Fax: 01868-723891

Norah and Ralph Brown

They laid the foundations for Grange Lodge in about 1698 and have been extending it ever since; the result is a harmonious whole, although tell-tale creaks from floorboards and varying ceiling heights are pointers to different eras. The house sits in three acres of very attractive garden, with 17 more acres surrounding the property. Ralph was out with hat and strimmer when I visited, seizing a weather window to keep the lawns immaculate. Nora and Ralph are a natural couple who laugh easily. There are two dining areas for the truly memorable food that has won the Browns a hatful of awards: A Taste of Ulster, The Galtee Breakfast and a British Airways award. Many of their vegetables, herbs and fruit are home-grown, and all are fresh as fresh. Then there's a very large drawing room in pale greens and pinks, and the cosy 'den' for those wet wintry evenings. Upstairs, bedrooms have thick carpets, ivy-crowded windows overlooking the garden, one very feminine with lacy bed hangings... but all different. A house of character, beautiful surroundings, outstandingly good food and a very warm welcome.

Rooms: 5: 3 doubles, 1 twin and 1 single: 3 with en suite shower, 1 with en/s bath and shower, 1 with hip-bath and shower.
Price: £34.50 p.p. Sing. supp. £14.50.
Breakfast: Included — full Irish.
Meals: Dinner from £22 à la carte.
Closed: December 20th — Feb 1st.

How to get there: From junction 15 on M1 take A29 towards Armagh/Moy. After 1 mile turn left at Grange, first right, house on the right.

Map Ref No: 8

Deans Hill
College Hill
Armagh
Co. Armagh
BT61 9DF

Tel: 01861-524923

Jill and Edward Armstrong

All those who wisely cross the border into Northern Ireland will want to drop in on historic Armagh, with its stunning cathedral. And Dean's Hill is a wonderful old house (1770) with its own mixed history. It sits on a hill at the end of a steep drive, surrounded by trees and looking down over school playing fields below. Inside the mood is intriguing, old-fashioned and elegant. Long white shutters block out the night, there's Georgian green paint on the walls, Georgian cornicing round the ceilings, frayed drapes on old sofas and piles of rugs on the floor. The bedrooms are extraordinary. One contains the tallest double bed I've ever seen and all the rooms are colossal with wooden floors, very pretty wallpaper and shuttered windows which look onto a wild garden. The most impressive of all has an old fireplace, wooden beds and huge overlapping rugs. The bathrooms are suitably large. This is an old-world family home where creaky floorboards and antique furnishings give the house a relaxed feeling of grandeur.

Rooms: 3: 1 four-poster with en suite bath; 1 twin with en suite bath; 1 single with private bath.
Price: £19 — £25 p.p. No single supplement.
Breakfast: Included — full Irish.
Meals: Restaurants in Armagh.
Closed: Christmas and New Year.

How to get there: Coming out of the centre of Armagh follow signs for the Planetarium. Dean's Hill is next stone entrance on left after Planetarium, with stone balls on pillars. If you reach Shell petrol station you've gone too far.

Map Ref No: 8

Clare
•
Donegal
•
Galway
•
Mayo
•
Sligo
•

The West Coast

Berry Lodge

Annagh, Spanish Point
Milltown Malbay
Co. Clare

Tel: 065-7087022
Fax: 065-7087022

Rita Meade

Driving through a howling wind that threatened to overturn my car I was beginning to hallucinate about fireplaces, hot food and smiley faces. Rita's friendly cocoon-by-the-sea couldn't have fitted the bill more exactly. Rita herself is self-deprecating, warm, cheerful and brimming with character — a fact well appreciated by the producers of her Clare FM radio cookery show. Cookery? Sorcery! The meal I had was perhaps the best I've eaten and certainly the best value I've had in Ireland. Everything from a mussels starter, through home-made sorbet, the lamb main course, choice of three puddings, excellence was piled on excellence. And only £18. Upstairs, pretty rooms look straight out to sea and on clear days you can even see it! They have deep low window-seats, firm orthopedic beds, warm colours with bright patchwork quilts, pretty blue curtains tied back, power showers, wooden floors, armchairs, soaps and shampoos, kitkats, tea, coffee, original fireplaces... you get the picture. Rita wants guests to like it here. Breakfast completely absorbed the taste buds and practically warranted the bill on its own.

Rooms: 5: 2 doubles and 3 triples, all with en suite showers.
Price: £18 — £23 p.p. Sing supp. £7.
Breakfast: Included — full Irish.
Meals: Restaurant dinners (7 — 10 pm): £18 — £22 (depending on season).
Closed: January 10th — February 14th.

How to get there: From Ennis take N85 signed to Inagh. Left in Inagh (R460) signed Milltown Malbay. In village take Killimer car ferry rd (N67), past Bellbridge Hotel, over the bridge, 2nd turn to the left. Berry Lodge is first house on right.

Old Parochial House

Cooraclare
Kilrush
Co. Clare

Tel: 065-9059059
Fax: 065-9051006
E-mail: oldparochial@webhead.ie.
www: www.webheads.ie/a/opc

Alyson and Sean O'Neill

Alyson and Sean bought this ecclesiastical house (1872) in 1986 and have done literally everything themselves — plumbing, wiring, painting, curtains. The house is painted in deep colours, grey/blue downstairs and blue, burgundy and green up. Bedrooms here are big with cornice or slatted wood ceilings, four-poster beds, wooden floors and views across fields. The whole place has a wholesome, busy, family feel and a sense of being among friends, however short your stay. This is not to say you will wake up with small children clambering all over you (!), although this IS a great place for families. Children will love the quiet riding pony, goats and hens which all roam around seeking attention. For those who need more independence they have converted the stable area into self-catering cottages with stone floors, wood beams and an open-plan top floor. Old Parochial House is a great place to escape the tumult of the city, to switch off — go for walks or to the beach or discover a little of the local scene. The village is a five-minute stroll and the pubs have good traditional music and seafood.

Rooms: 4: 2 doubles/twins sharing 1 shower; 1 double with en suite shower; 1 double/twin with en suite shower.
Price: £18 — £22.50 p.p. Sing. supp. £7.
Breakfast: Included — full Irish.
Meals: Good seafood available in pubs within 10 mins drive.
Closed: November 1st — April 1st.

How to get there: From Kilrush take R483 signed to Milltown Malbay for 4 miles. Through Cooraclare village, house signed 0.25 miles further on the left. From Lahinch thro' Quilty, house just before Cooraclare on RH side.

Fergus View
Kilnaboy
Corofin
Co. Clare

Tel: 065-6837606
Fax: 065-6837192
E-mail: deckell@indigo.ie

Mary and Declan Kelleher

In summer you can't actually see the River Fergus because of the vegetation. A large lawn and garden stretch in front of the house and beyond are the ruins of an Elizabethan fortress and medieval churchyard. Declan and Mary are keen to make you welcome. Great effort goes into your breakfast with crêpes, kippers and home-made porridge and they have produced a manual on the region which they love. This is the gateway to the famous Burren, an amazing lunar landscape of limestone slabs and home to a variety of rare flowers; your hosts are knowledgeable on the subject. They are also very 'up' on the Irish language and music; old original readers on phonetics and the like lie about, dating back to when this house was built as a teacher's residence. There is also a recently done-up self-catering cottage (sleeps five, £280 — £450 per week, Sat — Sat, not suitable for young children), with Swiss-chalet-style wood beams and fittings, sloping roofs in bedrooms and orthopaedic beds (all the beds at Fergus View are orthopaedic). This is a friendly family-run B&B with high standards and so close to the Burren.

Rooms: 6: 1 large family; 2 small family; 1 double; 1 double/twin: all with en suite shower. Also 1 double sharing bathroom.
Price: £20 p.p. Sing. supp. £7 — £11.
Breakfast: Included — full Irish.
Meals: Dinner £16 (3-course set menu). Wine list from £9.75 — £18.
Closed: Mid-October — Easter.

How to get there: From Shannon take N18 through Ennis to roundabout signed Ennistymon. 2 miles further right to Corofin — follow R476 to Corofin, on to Kilnaboy. House on left after ruined church.

Map Ref No: 11

Clifden House

Corofin
Co. Clare

Tel: 065-6837692
Fax: 065-6837692

Jim and Bernadette Robson

Since 1975 Jim and Bernadette have been painstakingly restoring this wonderful 1750s house themselves and, as Jim says, after that long it's quite clear what owns whom. This is a labour of love and they make no apology for any 'ramshackledom' encountered about the property by guests, such as the mottled façade and cracked mirrors in their antique frames. But that is not to say that what they have finished isn't lovely. The bedrooms have high ceilings and breathtaking views over Lake Inchiquin that you wouldn't know existed from the other side of the building. The lake runs right up to the house and meadow in front. Beyond it are the hills of the Burren, dotted with the odd cottage. The garden is a jungle of ferns and trees and there is a river which runs through a disused mill site. A wander through the fifteen acres at Clifden House is a romantic adventure, a paradise for children. Overgrown outbuildings, a self-catering stable wing, a treehouse, the ruins of a car... let serendipity be your guide. Come for interesting conversation, doing what you feel like, good food and an open door. Bernadette has a cat. And a dog.

Rooms: 4: 3 with en suite bathroom; 1 with en suite shower.
Price: £35 p.p. No sing. supp.
Breakfast: Included — full Irish.
Meals: Dinner £20 (notice by noon).
Closed: One month at Christmas.

How to get there: From Ennis take Ennistymon road, 2 miles out turn right to Corofin. Through village to shrine. Turn left, 2nd right, house signed up drive.

Map Ref No: 11

The Waterman's Lodge
Ballina
Killaloe
Co. Clare

Tel: 061-376333
Fax: 061-375445
E-mail: info@watermanslodge.ie
www: www.watermanslodge.ie

Tom Reilly

This riverside bungalow is big, comfy, clean and light. They must have been building to last in 1947, and with imagination too. The rooms are grouped around a gravel courtyard — great for tea out of the breeze, and a big atrium restaurant room with skylights has since been added. The hotel has plumped for king-size beds, walk-in wardrobes and glass-paned bathroom doors — "well, if you're sharing a room with someone...". The newness and layout of the building gives Watermans a little of the air of a private, slightly exclusive or continental suburban hotel — quiet, lightly reserved, perhaps a little naughtily indulgent — but the seagrass matting dispels any institutional feel. You really will be comfortable at Watermans — pampered even; you are in the village; you have a great view down onto the River Shannon — a short walk through fields, longer by road — and the ancient arches of the Ballina-Killaloe bridge (which is very historic in a complicated sort of way). *This is Tom's first year at the helm after a change of ownership and there are plans to become more wheelchair-friendly.*

Rooms: 10: 7 doubles and 3 twins: all en suite.
Price: £45 — £65 p.p. Sing. supp. £20.
Breakfast: Included — full Irish.
Meals: Dinner £28.50. Light lunches on request.
Closed: Never!

How to get there: From Limerick take N7 direction Dublin.12 miles after Limerick and just after Birdhill take left signed Killaloe/Ballina — 4 miles. Drive straight through (not across bridge). House on left as leaving village.

Map Ref No: 11

Danny Minnies Restaurant

Teach Killindarragh   **Tel:** 075-48201
Annagry, Rosses
Co. Donegal

Terri O'Donnell

The west coast of Donegal: a rugged deep green sea, white beaches and fertile hills thrilling with waterfalls and lakes. And the music: some of Ireland's best folk has emerged in local pubs and bars and burst onto the world stage. Enya and Clannad play often at Leo's down the road. It's a shame that everyone lives in white bungalows — they call it "Bungalow Blight". A real house is hard to find. So Terri took an old pub, painted it green, added a baronial, wood-panelled entrance gallery, several fireplaces (and an inglenook), exposed the dark old beams and made lots of extra space. Downstairs is now a celebrated restaurant, specialising in spanking fresh fish. With the parquet floor and low lighting it all has a well-designed homey feel — a relief from the kitsch. There must be a creative flair in her genes because both sons are musicians and paint well, and *everyone* cooks. The rooms are quirkily individual; one in tartan, another in bright green with an oriental feel. Beds are good and the breakfasts are a real treat. *Three miles from Donegal International Airport.*

Rooms: 5: 3 twins and 2 doubles: 2 have en suite baths; 3 rooms share a separate bathroom.
Price: £20 — £25 p.p. No sing. supp.
Breakfast: Included — full Irish.
Meals: Dinner à la carte about £20.
Closed: Jan 6th — Easter.

How to get there: From Letterkenny take N56 through Kilmacrenan. After 3 miles take left signed Glenveagh. Continue 13 miles and turn L on rejoining N56. 3 more miles, take Annaghry turning on R (R259). House in middle of village — big green building.

       Map Ref No: 1

Bruckless House

Bruckless
Dunkineely
Co. Donegal

Tel: 073-37071
Fax: 073-37070
E-mail: bruc@iol.ie
www: www.iol.ie/~bruc/bruckless.html.

Joan and Clive Evans

Life is mellow at Bruckless. The house revels in an extraordinary light, due mostly to the sea that surrounds it, but also to the height of the rooms and immaculate taste. The Evanses have brought back many lovely things from their years in the Orient: Chinese paintings done with a few perfectly simple brush strokes, beautiful rugs resting on the house's light wool carpets and a gorgeous rosewood table; old things too, like the chunky, Irish oak sideboard, deep-carved with fish and gargoyles, that Joan found in a peat store and laboriously cleaned. Your bedrooms are in the back — no privation though, for you are delightfully perched over a perfect time-warp of a cobbled courtyard. It is this that positively identifies the house as a classic Grange Farm in Georgian style (1745). The garden is an award-winning gem: lawns, flowers, a rockery and paths that meander through bluebells and rhododendrons past old Scots pines and maples to the rocky coast and along to the village. They are a Connemara Pony Stud Farm, keeping seven horses and some chickens on their 20 acres.

Rooms: 4: 1 twin and 1 double with en suite bathroom; 2 singles sharing 1 bathroom.
Price: £25 — £30 p.p.
Breakfast: Included — full Irish.
Meals: Not available.
Closed: October 1st — March 31st.

How to get there: From Donegal take N56 for Killybegs for 12 miles and go through Dunkineely. Bruckless House signposted on left after 2 miles.

Map Ref No: 1

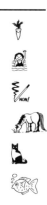

Bluebell Lodge

Inver
Co. Donegal

Tel: 073-36249
Fax: 073-36249

Dominique Grasset

This is a great area to explore. From Bluebell Cottage take long walks along the beaches or the River Eany (excellent for salmon fishing) where the ruins of an old monastery project eerily on a tidal promontory. There is also a secret and serene place on the woodland hill directly behind the lodge where the eponymous bluebells hold sway in spring. From here you have views over distant hills and the sea. The house itself is a converted stables and dairy house and very homely it has become. Dominique is flamboyantly nice, French and a school teacher. In the evenings and at weekends she puts her considerable enthusiasm into looking after her guests. You can come here to be "pampered" as Dominique puts it. This means massage, aromatherapy, facials and reflexology. Food here is fantastic too and not at all expensive — French in style with fresh herbs and veg from the garden. The whole house has a cosy sort of chaos which I found charming — books, drapes and a real log fire downstairs; geese and ducks outside; and small but quaint bedrooms upstairs. Come and be pampered.

Rooms: 3: 1 double with en suite shower; 1 double and single with en suite shower; 1 twin with downstairs bath.
Price: £20 — £25 p.p. Pampering weekends £155.
Breakfast: Included — Irish, Continental or vegetarian.
Meals: Dinner (3 or 4 courses) £14-£18.
Closed: Never!

How to get there: From Donegal Town take N56 towards Killybegs — house signed 9 miles on left just before River Eany.

Map Ref No: 1

Smuggler's Creek Inn

Rossnowlagh
Co. Donegal

Tel: 072-52366

Conor Britton

The city crowd come from far away for the *craic* at Smuggler's Creek. Soft-suited and spoken, with a kind word for young staff, local restaurateur Conor hit on the idea of the 'destination' pub with rooms. The old cliff-top inn has been done up and over — and with impressive results. A heavily-timbered bar with joists, stone floors, pillars and log-burning fire is cluttered with diverting, mainly nautical, bric-à-brac and plays host to frequent (unplugged) music sessions. Hearty, flushed groups eat and drink well at rough pine tables. The oysters await your pleasure in a corner aquarium. The conservatory and restaurant are more mannered, still busy, but less boisterous, particularly the latter with a quiet, near country-house feel and light wood floors. There is a great emphasis on food here — Conor started as a chef — and seafood dominates an inventive smuggler-themed menu. And then the rooms — bright, snug and cottagey with real fresh charm and expansive Atlantic or Blue Stack Mountain views. If you can get a balcony so much the better. You may need the smack of a salty breeze the morning after a night downstairs.

Rooms: 5: all doubles: 2 with en suite bathrooms; 3 with en suite shower.
Price: £27.50 p.p. Sing. supp. £10.
Breakfast: Included — full Irish.
In restaurant about £17 à la carte. Set lunch on Sundays £12.50.
Closed: November 20th — December 26th.

How to get there: From Donegal take N15 direction Sligo for 6 miles. Take turning to Rossnowlagh on right. Right again in village. Follow signs — Smuggler's Creek on clifftop headland after 1 mile.

Map Ref No: 1

Portnason House

Portnason
Ballyshannon
Co. Donegal

Tel: 072-52016
Fax: 072-52016

Madge Sharkey

It is always interesting when a strong design conviction is given reign in a house as grand as this. Madge, an art and design graduate, has been slowly building up Portnason — the result is a striking, refreshing whole. She likes fresh colours and hates clutter — with a near Mediterranean purity; wooden floors are stripped or painted in pastel shades and bright tile fireplaces warm the cool spaces. No ancient window-tax blocks off the light here; it falls freely on flagstones, Laura Ashley papers and a mulberry staircase that rises into a wide-planked hall. There is plenty of space in bedrooms of blond wood and wicker, cotton dhurries on the floor and cotton quilts on brass beds. White wooden shutters open to golden views of the Erne estuary and dunes beyond. The cast-iron, claw-footed baths have been re-enamelled to gleaming whiteness and one bedroom has a stair leading to a loft bathroom where you can soak under the sun. The neatly-walled grounds stretch away to a nature reserve pond — home to waterhens and last year an itinerant flamingo. There are boats and wetsuits for waterskiing, and private access to long estuarine walks, sea and beaches.

Rooms: 8: 5 doubles, 2 twins and 1 kingsize: all with en suite baths or showers or both.
Price: £35 — £45 p.p. Sing. supp. £10.
Breakfast: Included — full Irish.
Meals: Available locally in many excellent restaurants.
Closed: November 1st — March 31st.

How to get there: From Donegal take N15 direction Sligo. The house is down a long mature sycamore-lined avenue — driveway on right after Ballyshannon at stone gate lodge.

Map Ref No: 1

Rhu-Gorse

Lough Eske
Donegal Town
Co. Donegal

Tel: 073-21685
Fax: 073-21685
E-mail: rhugorse@iol.ie

Gráinne McGettigan

Sturdily stone-built in 1983, Rhu-Gorse is neatly sunk into the valleyside and overlooks from some height magnificent Lough Eske and the Blue Stack Mountains where the sun rises. The joists are pitch pine and exposed, the walls rough rendered, while the chairs are soft and the fire burns warmly. An unusual hall is staged on three levels and rises with the stairs to big, frill-free bedrooms with stunning views and steaming baths. I slept well here. There is little pretension or pose — this is a working house where Gráinne (pronounced Gronyer) raises her four children and stables five brood mares. That doesn't stop her freshly squeezing your orange juice in the morning, though, and making sure you have plenty of logs if you want to sit up late at the hearth. Or sit out on the sun terrace watching the foals frolic in the paddock. Any kids will love to frolic too in the soft, hummocky garden and there is a tennis court. Down by the lake lurks a primeval oak forest — a protected site — so walk with care.

Rooms: 3: 1 family with en suite bathroom; 1 twin with en suite shower; 1 double with private bathroom.
Price: £22.50 — £25 p.p. Sing. supp. £5.
Breakfast: Included — full Irish.
Meals: Harvey's Point Country Hotel is very close.
Closed: November 1st — Easter.

How to get there: From Donegal take N56 direction Killybegs. 0.25 miles to sign on right "Lough Eske". Follow signs for Harvey's Point for 2.7 miles to crossroads, then left, go 2.5 miles — house on right.

Map Ref No: 2

Ardnamona
Lough Eske
Co. Donegal

Tel: 073-22650
Fax: 073-22819

Kieran and Annabel Clarke

Deep in the rhododendron forest, logs are popping on the Ardnamona fires. Annabel is in the kitchen with her two toddlers, coolly working a delicious magic. Is Kieran in the woods, transforming a one-time arboretum to National Heritage status, or tuning a friend's piano ("it was a great job in '60s London, Paul McCartney in the morning and Alfred Brendel in the afternoon...")? That could be him in the loft-gallery music room, eking out Beethoven on Paderewsky's Steinway. Actually, what Kieran really likes to do is sit up late and talk. We were animated on the aesthetics of taste, style and mass culture. Ardnamona lends itself to long, cosy, convivial evenings; pine floors with gracefully aged rugs lead one room to another, the fire radiates at knee height and dark velvet curtains keep the night at bay. Morning breaks in cheerful and feminine bedrooms — white-painted furniture, patchwork quilts and, for some, window seats with views over the Lough to the heather-cloaked Blue Stack Mountains. The conservatory sparkles with a sea mosaic and you may stroll through bluebells to the lake and take a boat — or swim!

Rooms: 6: 3 doubles with en suite bathrooms; 1 double and 2 twins with private bathroom.
Price: £35 — £45 p.p. Sing. supp. £10.
Breakfast: Included — full Irish.
Meals: Dinner £20 (3 courses).
Closed: Never but advance booking essential.

How to get there: From Donegal N15 direction Letterkenny for 2.5 miles. Then take small turning on L marked Harvey's Point Country Hotel/Lough Eske Drive. Straight on for 5 miles. Low wall then white-gated drive on right.

Map Ref No: 2

Gortfad
Castlefinn
Co. Donegal

Tel: 074-46135

Dolly Taylor

When you sit out in the bay windows of Dolly's big front bedrooms, you feel as if you're sitting in the garden — an oasis of comfort and colour in a patchwork of fields, pastures and hedgerows spreading to the far-off mountains. This is the perfect place to read the paper — cosy and familiar. Dolly's is a touch of rural grace at a keen price. Breakfast with silver napkin rings in front of a glowing stove among her late husband's racing trophies. She's a warm and wise lady, always ready to laugh. She'll not take you up to the upper farm to dig for gold — as legend has it you'll lose the use of your hands. She'd rather chat or play cards. The Taylor family has inhabited this Edwardian/Victorian house for seven generations so it's full of old possessions and atmosphere. The antique beds are soft and free of the expected lumps and the house is full of fresh flowers and books, one of which will probably end up in your lap by the sitting room fire.

Rooms: 4: 1 family, 2 twins and 1 double: all with en suite shower.
Price: £16 — £18 p.p. Occasional sing. supp. £5.
Breakfast: Included — full Irish.
Meals: Good food 5 miles away at Keys Hotel.
Closed: Mid-September — mid-March.

How to get there: From Donegal take N15 through Ballybofey and Castlefinn. As you leave Castlefinn (just at end of speed limit sign) turn left. After 0.5 miles house is signed on right. It is 200 yards up a hedged drive.

Map Ref No: 2

Ardeen
Ramelton
Co. Donegal

Tel: 074-51243
Fax: 074-51243

Anne and Bert Campbell

Ardeen sits squarely on the River Lennon just as it flows into Lough Swilly. From your comfortable big room you should be able to see salmon leaping. If feeling active you could play tennis; they are keen on that here and have newly surfaced their court. Anne and Bert are a good couple to sit with by the fire — masters of the lightly-amused approach to living, they make a naturally hospitable team. Bridge players are always welcome. The house is tidy, everything spick and span. Anne made the quilts and lampshades and has turned the old nursery into a charming, pine-floored single suite with blue gingham and shower. And then Ramelton, a beautiful Irish Heritage village of stone, narrow hill, winding lanes and pubs. Try "Conways", hard by the old brick warehouses on the quay. This hole-in-the-wall with dark, smoke-stained wood panelling, flagged floors, murky light, massive coal fires and old whiskey vats is 'the business'.

Rooms: 5: 1 single with en suite shower;1 double and 1 family with en/s shower; 1 double and 1 twin sharing 1 bathroom.
Price: £18 — £20 p.p.
Breakfast: Included — full Irish.
Meals: Not available.
Closed: October 31st — Easter.

How to get there: From Derry N13 right at end of dual carriageway approaching Letterkenny. Follow signs to Ramelton for 7 miles. Go down hill to river, turn right and follow river to Ardeen, 0.25 miles on right.

Map Ref No: 2

Croaghross

Portsalon
Letterkenny
Co. Donegal

Tel: 074-59548
Fax: 074-59548
E-mail: jkdeane@iol.ie
www: http://www.bigfoot.com/~croaghross/

John and Kay Deane

A tiny lane takes you up past the holiday bungalows to John and Kay's more substantial, carefully-designed, single-floor home. They holidayed up here for 20 years so they knew what they wanted. It has all worked out; the patio rooms open up towards the sea, there is a little kitchenette (for your snacks, champagne and fresh milk), facilities for the disabled, a drying room and the work of local artists exhibited in the halls. Kay loves cooking on the Aga (she devours cookbooks) and only uses the very best local produce — wild salmon, butcher's sausages and naturally squeezed orange juice. The dried peels serve as an aromatic firelighter in the parlour. No one will rush you at breakfast; they leave guests to find their own pace. You might call John laid back, while Kay seems more energetic, but both are cheerful and very happy to have you. Kay's mother, who lives just up the hill, is a gardener, so there are fresh flowers all around and a lovely lawn. They also let a new cottage — bright with pine, blue check and cosy with a stone fireplace.

Rooms: 5: 1 family en suite bath; 1 twin en/s bath; 1 twin en/s shower; 1 double en/s bath; 1 double en/s shower.
Price: £20 — £30 p.p. Sing. supp. £5.
Breakfast: Included — full Irish.
Meals: Dinner £15.
Closed: November 1st — March 12th.
Out of season reservations by arrangement.

How to get there: Just before Letterkenny turn R to Ramelton — 4 miles. L at bottom of hill and L again after bridge to Milford — 4 miles. Before Milford turn R to Fanad/Kerrykeel. thro' Kerrykeel, signs to Portsalon. R at crossroads. 0.5 miles take lane on L opposite entrance to golf clubhouse.

Map Ref No: 2

Glen House

Straid
Clonmany
Co. Donegal

Tel: 077-76745

Doris Russo

The Inishowen peninsula is one of Donegal's showpieces with its beautiful sandy bays and pristine beaches. Georgian Glen House was built in 1766 by O'Flaherty (who married vicar Chichester's daughter) on land given as her dowry. It is named after the glen it stands in, complete with river and 30-ft waterfall. When Doris arrived there from New Jersey it was a "pile of rubble". She bought "history and location and that's it!" She kept what she could (shutters, thick walls, sash windows); the rest is Doris, an achievement made more difficult by the ghosts of a sea captain and a young girl. At least one workman refused to come back. Today there is a 'ghost corner' for children to play in. The style is American with country pine, recliners, landscape pictures and carpets all coming from the USA; and breakfast is American too with maple syrup and pancakes, omelettes, fresh fruit, French toast, muffins, American coffee. One quote from a Polish lady who visited: "I thought I'd died and gone to heaven" — high praise indeed. The bedrooms are uncluttered, with flowery bedspreads, but you come here for the outdoors. Doris loves walking and will point you in the right direction, whether its mountain or beach.

Rooms: 2: 1 twin and 1 double, both with en suite shower.
Price: £18 p.p. Sing supp. £2.
Breakfast: Included — American.
Meals: Dinner £10 by arrangement. Picnic hampers available too.
Closed: Never!

How to get there: From Derry A2 direction Buncrana. Right in Buncrana signs to Clonmany. Through village and bear left over bridge then bear right, following signs to Glen House. House 0.5 miles on left.

Map Ref No: 2

Delphi Lodge
Leenane
Co. Galway

Tel: 095-42211
Fax: 095-42296
E-mail: delfish@iol.ie
www:
http://mayo_ireland.ie/delphi.htm

Peter Mantle

The above photo gives a good idea of what to expect at Delphi. It had been recommended to me from Rosslare round to Galway. Originally built by the Marquis of Sligo in the mid-1830s as a fishing lodge, the house presides over 600 acres of land and 1000 acres of water, bog, mountain and rock. Fishing is still a priority; the fisherpeople provide the colour and everyone else stops them talking of nothing else! This is important as guests all dine together at a long table with Peter helming the meal each evening. No one is forced to eat 'in' but these meals can often be enormously entertaining and the atmosphere is strictly house party. By the time you leave you really do feel as if these are your friends and this is your house and it's only a matter of time before you're back. Conversation flows throughout the house. Food is wonderful and all the rooms uncluttered: long mirrors, proper bathrooms and no gimmicks. And, of course, the wonderful view of Fin Lough. Delphi lies in the heart of Connemara and I imagine hearty walks in winter with one eye on the library fire and a stiff drink back at Delphi.

Rooms: 12: all doubles with en suite bathrooms.
Price: £30 — £60 p.p. Sing. supp. £20.
Breakfast: Included — full Irish.
Meals: Dinner £29. Lunch £8. Packed lunches £8.
Closed: Mid-December — mid-January.

How to get there: From Clifden follow signs to Westport and Leenane. 3 miles after Leenane turn left (signed Delphi). Follow for 6 miles along coast. House in woods on left 0.5 miles after Delphi Adventure Centre.

Map Ref No: 5

GALWAY

Killary Lodge

Leenane
Co. Galway

Tel: 095-42276/42245
Fax: 095-42314
E-mail: killary@iol.ie
www: www.iol.ie/killary/

Jamie and Mary Young

Killary Lodge is a playground for the still-active in (yet another!) idyllic Connemara setting. Completely surrounded by hills, the Lodge sits right on Killary Harbour and a bog that attracts a rich wildlife — schools of dolphins, sea otters, seals that preen themselves on the bay's island right in front of the house. And the area teems with birds. Jamie and Mary and a young, friendly (and, I imagine, fit by the end of the season) staff do more than is necessary to ensure that guests get as much out of the experience as possible. There are an 'honesty' bar and shop, dinners are candlelit, great efforts are made to cater for different dietary needs and all the food is made right here. Rooms are comfortably furnished with hand-made beechwood furniture throughout but no televisions as a matter of policy. A wonderful place just to read a book, chat to other guests or merely to sit and soak up the view. There is also an array of professionally organized activities on offer: catamaran sailing, cycling, kayaking, water-skiing and hill-walking.

Rooms: 20: range of doubles/twins/singles/triples/family: all with en suite bath or shower.
Price: £29 — £37 p.p. Sing. supp. £15 — £20.
Breakfast: Included — full Irish.
Meals: Dinner £19 (B,B and D deals available). Packed lunches £4. Snack menu lunches.
Closed: Christmas and New Year.

How to get there: From Galway follow signs to Clifden (N59). Turn right at Maam Cross then left at Maam. Follow signs to Leenane, through village in direction of Clifden. House 4 miles out on right.

Map Ref No: 5

Rose Cottage

Rockfield
Moyard near Clifden
Co. Galway

Tel: 095-41082
Fax: 095-41082
E-mail: conamara@indigo.ie

Patricia Shanley-O'Toole

Rose Cottage is surrounded by rolling pastures for sheep and cattle and has 48 acres of its own, farmed by Patricia's father. But one of the greatest draws is the sheer loveliness — mountains, lakes and all — that is Connemara; the Twelve Pins National Park is just two and a half miles up the road. For man-made breath-removal visit amazing lakeside Kylemore Abbey, only five miles away. Patricia has taken over Rose Cottage from her parents and greets her guests with grace and enthusiasm. She is particularly keen on traditional Irish food and everything is made on site. The house itself is 170 years old with extensions which give some parts of the house a more modern feel. But essentially the place is very countrified, with stone and wood floors, a nice drawing room with peat fire which Patricia will light for you, matting on the stairs, white painted walls... and lots of wood. Bedrooms are in cheery colours with wood fittings and windows in sloping walls. This is not a house for TV. It's a warm hideaway where you will be fed wholesome meals, sit before real fires and, if you've any strength at all, struggle up at least one Connemaran hill!

Rooms: 8: 2 triples, 4 doubles and 2 twins: all with en suite shower.
Price: £18 — £20 p.p. No sing. supp.
Breakfast: Included — full Irish.
Meals: Dinner £16 — £18. Packed lunches £5.
Closed: November 1st — March 1st.

How to get there: From Clifden take Westport Rd (N59) for 6 miles — Rose Cottage signed 2 miles after Cleggan turning on right. Do not take the Cleggan turn!

Map Ref No: 5

The Quay House

Beach Road
Clifden
Co. Galway

Tel: 095-21369
Fax: 095-21608
E-mail: thequay@iol.ie

Julia and Patrick Foyle

Most people visit Clifden at some point in their Connemaran peregrinations and it is a relief that somewhere as special as the Quay House exists to make staying there an extra joy. Just out of town, this lovely 1820s house sits right on Clifden Bay and is special for any number of reasons. Common features in rooms are fantastic mirrors that add depth to the rooms, white-shuttered windows, and painted wooden boards for walls. One room has a little balcony, one a four-poster with red tassles, and all look straight onto the working fishing boats that tie up in the bay outside the house. Julia is English, Paddy Irish, and they have that magic touch which effortlessly relaxes people and encourages rapport between guests. There have been a few changes this year and now dinners are at the excellent Foyle-owned Destry's in town. New rooms have been added and my heart sank when I first heard this. I needn't have worried. They're just as generous in proportion and enticing as the older rooms. Also this year Paddy's lunches in the leafy conservatory (and outside on hot days) will happen. He has promised.

Rooms: 14: 2 triples; 2 family; 10 doubles/twins: all with en suite bathrooms.
Price: From £35 p.p. Sing. supp. £10 (dependent on season).
Breakfast: Included — full Irish.
Meals: Packed lunches £5. Lunch from £7.50 (open to the public).
Closed: November 1st — March 17th.

How to get there: In Clifden take beach road down the hill from the centre of town. The Quay House is 500 yards on the right.

Map Ref No: 5

Currarevagh House

Oughterard
Connemara
Co. Galway

Tel: 091-552312
Fax: 091-552731

Harry and June Hodgson

After a hot bath, I sat on the lawn in front of Currarevagh, gin and tonic in hand, letting the fresh air cool me and drinking in the breathtaking setting: the garden and 150 acres of woodland behind, crystal clear Lough Corrib and its islands in front. There can be nothing to mar the experience. The scene invites boating from the house's jetty, although the frequent shallows require some experience if you use a motor. Or just go rowing — but stay awake, the lake is 30 miles long! Inside the house you will be greeted with easy-mannered smiles by Harry or June and shown your room with a quick explanation that there are no rules except turning up on time for dinner — at 8 o'clock sharp. If you've eaten here before, you'll be ready well in advance. June prestidigitates in the kitchen. Not just plain and good, creative and wonderful. My starter was a grapefruit soufflé, light as air, followed by bass in lemon sauce, duck roulade, mocha, all perfect. Guests eat separately but come together for coffee by the fire on comfortable sofas in the drawing room. Bedrooms vary (room 1 is wonderful with great lake views) — all in all this is a very special place indeed.

Rooms: 15: 2 singles; 13 doubles/twins: 13 with en suite bath and 2 with en suite shower.
Price: £49 p.p. Sing. supp. £17.50.
Breakfast: Included — full Irish.
Meals: Dinner £21.
Closed: Mid-October — Easter.

How to get there: From Oughterard take the Glann Lakeshore Rd (signed to house from Oughterard). 4 miles, house on right.

Map Ref No: 5

38

Fough East

Oughterard
Connemara
Co. Galway

Tel: 091-552614 or 091-552957
Fax: 091-552465
E-mail: clearvu@iol.ie

James and Christa McGeough

I liked everything about this little B&B. James and Christa are a natural, easy-going, chatty, even therapeutic, young couple and their brand new B&B house has been specially designed for simple comfort. Polished wooden floors and firm beds, smallish but simply designed rooms with plain yellow walls and bright bed covers and cupboard-style showers... everything gleams, works, is comfortable and warm. Christa runs a kindergarten by day (she's German so she calls it a 'play school'!) and her own young son may welcome you too. James works with his father in the high-class butcher's across the road and the benefits of this are apparent at breakfast — excellent sausages and the first black or white pudding I've ever enjoyed. The breakfast makes Fough East (rhymes with 'cow beast') good value on its own. You're right in the middle of Oughterard here, an ever-more popular place to base yourself for Connemara, Galway City, the Aran Islands — and there's plenty of good eating in town for your dinner. I wholeheartedly recommend James and Christa to you.

Rooms: 5: 2 family, 3 doubles, all with en suite shower.
Price: £17 p.p. Sing supp £4.
Breakfast: Included — full Irish or Continental.
Meals: Lots of restaurants in town.
Closed: October 1st — June.

How to get there: From Galway take N59 north to Oughterard — right in town centre, house 100m on right.

Camillaun

Eighterard, Oughterard
Connemara
Co. Galway

Tel: 091-552678
Fax: 091-552439
E-mail: camillaun@tinet.ie
www: http://camillaunfishing@tinet.ie

Deirdre and Greg Forde

Greg and Deirdre pinpointed where they wanted a house, bought a plot and built a house: a warm, modern, family home with real fires, simple but attractive furnishings... and the River Owenriff as next-door neighbour. The garden runs down to Greg's home-made jetties where his seven boats are moored in season. Fisherpeople take these down river for a mile or so and out into Lough Corrib — ghillies are available. It's a big lake with brown trout, salmon, perch and pike. And for picnics there's always Inchagoill Island with its two monasteries. Greg (fishing) and Deirdre (teaching) are a young couple with one young son and the atmosphere at Camillaun is cheerful and involving. Upstairs rooms in the house look over the garden with its azaleas and rhododendron and, of course, the river (you can always hear it burbling). The rooms are simply done with wood floors and plain-coloured rugs, bright colours, the odd antiquey piece... but nothing is overdone. Simple comfort in a lively household with very friendly people. Just as B&B is meant to be. *The tennis court looked as if it might be ready by the time this is published!*

Rooms: 4: 1 twin with en suite bath; 1 twin with en suite shower; 1 family and 1 double sharing 1 bath.
Price: £16.50 — £18 p.p. Sing supp. £6. Full board (B&B, packed lunch, dinner: £34 — £35.50).
Breakfast: Included — full Irish.
Meals: Dinner £13.50.
Closed: September 30th — Easter.

How to get there: From Galway take N59 north into Oughterard. Turn right in centre, then first left over bridge. House signed 200m on right down side road.

Map Ref No: 5

Lisdonagh House

Caherlistrane
Co. Galway

Tel: 093-31163
Fax: 093-31528
E-mail: lisdonagh@iol.ie
www: http://www.galway-guide.com/pages/lisdonagh

John and Finola Cooke

Lisdonagh is a find. It really is! Prepare yourself for tiny lanes. When you finally arrive you are confronted with a grand, early Georgian house on the shore of Lough Hackett, in 250 acres of walkable farmland and woodland. There isn't a hint of the world you've just left. Some of the interior features are just as stunning, not least the oval entrance hall with its 1790 murals, the new curved panelling in the oval 'honesty' bar and the magnificent staircase which winds down in satisfying arcs to the 'basement'. Everything has been recently refurbished and you'd be pushed to find anything more comfortable in a 5-star hotel. Stylish, uncluttered rooms have marble-tiled bathrooms, some with lovely views of the lake, but perhaps the jewel in the crown is the new pavilion room. This is only Lisdonagh's second season and restoration plans are afoot for the walled garden. To top it all John and Finola are such nice, relaxed hosts and the food is spectacular, with great emphasis laid on organic produce. The basic philosophy here is home-from-home. If only! *Self-catering in gate lodge at £250 — £300 a week.*

Rooms: 10: 9 doubles/twins, 3 with en suite shower, 7 with en suite bath; 1 family with en suite bath.
Price: £47 — £57 p.p. Sing. supp. £20.
Breakfast: Included — full Irish.
Meals: Dinner £25 at 8 pm. Packed lunches for fishermen.
Closed: December and January.

How to get there: From Galway take N17 towards Sligo. After 16 miles turn left towards Headford/Caherlistrane. In Caherlistrane turn right at Queally's pub, go 2 more miles before turning left, signed down narrow lane.

Map Ref No: 6

Cregg Castle

Corrandulla
Co. Galway

Tel: 091-791434
Fax: 091-791434 (daytime)
E-mail: creggcas@indigo.ie
www: indigo.ie/~creggcas

Ann Marie and Pat Broderick

Cregg Castle must be among the most laid-back places in Ireland. Built in 1648, it was originally one of the many large houses owned by the ubiquitous Kirwan family; despite its grand presence in 165 acres of park and farmland, there is a faded, down-to-earth, even down-at-heel, feeling to the interior. Huge rooms are furnished with a miscellany of original antiques such as the curtains and pelmets in the dining room and the candelabra in the drawing room... and then there are the big old worn sofas and chairs that surround an open fire. Rooms upstairs vary considerably — some are enormous with lovely views over the surrounding woodland. Eccentricity reigns here, but in the most welcoming way. Ann Marie and Pat are both players of traditional Irish music and this is a very important aspect to the house. There are no rules and the hope is you will slow down to the Brodericks' pace of life as it is lived in this monument to a bygone age. Children love the animals and the freedom to explore, adults the peace, music and fireside chat. Fishing is on Lough Corrib (five miles) and the River Clare (just two). Don't come for luxury — come for a bit of atmosphere.

Rooms: 7: 2 family suites with en suite bath; 1 family with en/s shower; 3 doubles with en/s shower; 1 double with private shower.
Price: £25 — £30 p.p. Sing. supp. £10.
Breakfast: Included — full Irish.
Meals: Dinner £16. Wine from £9 — £16.
Closed: November 1st — March 7th.

How to get there: From Galway take N17 towards Sligo. After 7 miles turn left signed Corandulla. Another 3 miles, gates and sign on left.

Gardenfield House

Tuam
Co. Galway

Tel: 093-24865
Fax: 093-24601

Michael and Esther Mannion

I was a bit of a disappointment when I arrived at Gardenfield as two small children had hoped I was the man with the ducks. However, we buried our differences and made quite a large entourage as we did the tour. The kids wanted to show me everything, while Esther apologized for their enthusiasm. No apology required. I was introduced to a mob of sheep doing their bit by mowing the front lawn and the children's hens who were helping out with the breakfast. And two ponies. The house was built in 1860 and is now a busy family farmhouse with Michael farming 56 acres of sheep and cow. Upstairs all is clean and light and homely with slate fireplaces, warm, dark colours, wooden shutters, the odd teddy bear — all in all there is a lived-in feel that permeates the whole house. Everything for dinner is home-made and Esther uses her discretion about communal dining. If you want to take care of yourself they have converted some stables at the back of the house which are stone-flagged, with exposed walls and nicely finished in wood... all very comfortable. Fishermen head down to the River Clare that runs through their land. Ask about pets.

Rooms: 3: 1 twin with own bathroom; 1 twin with own shower room; 1 double with en suite shower.
Price: £18 — £20 p.p. Sing. supp. £4 (discretionary).
Breakfast: Included — full Irish.
Meals: Dinner £16. Packed lunch £4.
Closed: Never!

How to get there: From Galway take N17 towards Sligo to Tuam (20 miles). Continue past town; 1 mile after lights, signed left to Gardenfield Hse. Follow signs from there (about 1.5 miles in total).

Map Ref No: 6

Castle ffrench

Ballinamore Bridge
Co. Galway

Tel: 0903-22288
Fax: 0903-22003

Bill and Sheila Bagliani

When dinner is served it is not unusual for guest to have travelled 30 miles or more to the gates, then another mile up the avenue to the house itself. The Castle, as it is known locally, appears suddenly round a curve, a huge solid block built in 1779 by Sir Charles ffrench, replacing an earlier castle. Set in rolling parkland this is a listed Georgian house with its elaborate plasterwork carefully restored. Blazing turf fires, huge bedrooms and good food are the hallmarks of this very rural country house. There are still some rooms to be refurbished but those they have finished are delightful and the house is chock-full of eye-catching features — vaulted semi-basement, ornate cornicing, marble fireplaces, wooden floors, flagstoned hallway, barrel-ceilinged corridors. The bedrooms have thick rugs, the odd tapestry and they come with giant bathrooms too. The house is surrounded by its own light woods and paddocks and the views improve as you climb. Horses are an important issue at Castle ffrench. There is also good trout fishing in nearby rivers, or you might prefer a walk through a genuine Irish bog. Bill is a keen carriage driver and breeds Arabian horses, while Sheila is horse woman and artist. *Art and painting courses available.*

Rooms: 4: 2 with en suite bath; 2 with private bath.
Price: £45 p.p. Sing supp. £20.
Breakfast: Included — full Irish.
Meals: Dinner £24 with 24 hours notice.
Closed: Mid-October — 1st April.

How to get there: From Ballinasloe take Tuam Road to Ahascragh. Through village past Statoil garage for 1 mile to school. Turn R signed Ballygar. 3 miles to entrance gates on R-hand side. Drive up avenue for 1 mile.

Map Ref No: 6

Man of Aran Cottage

Inishmor
Aran Islands
Co. Galway

Tel: 099-61301
Fax: 099-61301

Maura and Joe Wolfe

The Aran Islands get very popular in summer so I would recommend visiting on a wild winter day or, better, during the months of April, May, September, October. If you do (and I urge you to) then seek out Man of Aran Cottage, even if you can't stay. The house was built in the 1930s for the interior shots of Robert Flaherty's documentary film on the islands, "Man of Aran" (a couple of French film buffs turned up while I was there). Perfect location right by the sea. And then there are Maura and Joe who are so relaxed and friendly that you could see people visibly unwind as they stooped through the door. Maura had cyclists drying by the open fire while she dished up hot soups. All their food is home-spun and Joe is a self-confessed vegetable maniac. It's all organic and while Maura cooks, Joe does the salads: "It's the only artistic inclination I have," he says. Thick, white-painted stone walls enclose the restaurant and the three charming little rooms. They will let the whole place out in winter. This is the perfect little hideaway. Go and write your first novel there.

Rooms: 3: 1 twin and 1 double sharing 1 bathroom; 1 double with own shower room.
Price: £18 — £21 p.p. Sing. supp. £7 (high season only).
Breakfast: Included — full Irish.
Meals: Dinner £16 — £19. Lunch £1.90 — £7. Packed lunches available.
Closed: Not often!

How to get there: From Galway take the Spiddal Road to Rossaveen. Take a ferry and hire a mini-bus or bike on arrival.

45

Map Ref No: 10

Fermoyle Lodge
Casla (Costelloe)
Connemara
Co. Galway

Tel: 091-786111
Fax: 091-786154

Nicola Stronach

Driving along the hill road between Oughterard and Costelloe you would be forgiven for thinking that you had somehow gone seriously wrong. There is nothing for miles but bare hill and distant lake below. But persevere, for eventually an oasis will heave into sight, a 19th-century fishing lodge surrounded by trees that by rights shouldn't be there. And inside the house an extremely friendly couple, he French, she English (children too), who have bought and done up this lovely old house. There is a huge open-plan hall, two sitting rooms, all with pale green walls... and the dining room is enormous, giving onto a gravel terrace where you can dine if the weather permits. And the views from there are stunning. From a height you look over a network of lakes and uninterrupted mountainscape — and I mean uninterrupted. The house is remarkably secluded. They are still untangling the garden which is full of rhododendron and palm. There is a covered tunnel-avenue, an old stone staircase and a path that leads down to the nearest lake. You will be well looked after at Fermoyle — comfortable rooms with spectacular views, warm (even in winter), good food and natural hosts.

Rooms: 5: 2 twins, 2 doubles and 1 single: all with en suite bath.
Price: £38 p.p. Sing. supp. £10.
Breakfast: Included — full Irish.
Meals: Dinner £22. Picnic lunches £7 for fisherpeople.
Closed: Never! Booking essential.

How to get there: From Galway take N59 to Oughterard. Turn left in town (very small road) to Costelloe (Casla in Irish). Fermoyle Lodge 11 miles on right amongst trees.

Moycullen House

Moycullen
Co. Galway

Tel: 091-555566 or 091-555621
Fax: 091-555566

Marie and Philip Casburn

Drive over wild moorland between the coast and Moycullen and up a long drive to this unusual 'arts and crafts' style house, built in the late 1800s. Set in 33 acres of dense jungly gardens, it has views straight over Lough Corrib and at night you can even see the lights of distant Galway City. The garden itself is a tangle of rhododendron, rowan tree, bamboo and then boggy woodland — a child's paradise. Inside, though, there's been substantial rearrangement at Moycullen since the last edition and all for the better say well-nourished locals. The house has been successfully transformed downstairs into a buzzy little restaurant with rooms; walls have been exposed, brick fireplaces revealed, wooden tables set out. Philip and Marie's son Richard has taken over as chef and, with his wife Louise, produces great Irish food with seafood a speciality. Upstairs, the rooms remain as unusual and enticing as before — generous spaces with complicated wood-framed angles, great views, free-standing bath — the master room is certainly the most impressive. Highly recommended on all fronts.

Rooms: 3: 1 family with en suite bath; 1 twin with private bath; 1 family with private shower.
Price: £35 — £40 p.p. Sing. supp. £10.
Breakfast: Included — full Irish.
Meals: Dinner (7 — 9.30, book ahead): à la carte, main courses from £10.
Closed: 3 days at Christmas, mid-January — end of February.

How to get there: From Galway take N59 (Clifden Rd) into Moycullen — left at crossroads, 1 mile up hill. House signed on left up drive.

Map Ref No: 10

Killeen House

Killeen
Bushypark
Co. Galway

Tel: 091-524179
Fax: 091-528065

Catherine Doyle

One of many wonderful Galway houses that sit beside lakes, Killeen House looks over Lough Corrib; the well-tended garden leads down past some old ruined walls to the water's edge, a ten minute walk. The setting is wonderful and is a good base for visiting Connemara. The house itself is 1840s with a more recent extension and is owned and run by a very characterful Catherine who genuinely enjoys the company of her guests. She has put a huge amount of energy into the house, particularly the bedrooms. Each is themed, often along English lines — Victorian, Edwardian, Regency, etc — and where possible the furniture and furnishings reflect this. Deep thick carpets (all locally hand-made) lie over wood floors and under massive new comfortable beds, often strapping seven-footers, and there is plenty of space. Downstairs, the sitting room is formal-elegant with four high-backed armchairs pointing in to a coffee-table on an octagonal rug on parquet floors, and in the dining room three tables can be used for communal or separate dining. A most beautiful spot.

Rooms: 5: all double with en suite bathroom (1 with shower only).
Price: £35 — £45 p.p. Sing. supp. £20.
Breakfast: Included — full Irish.
Meals: Not available but 'Drimcong', one of Ireland's best restaurants, is just down the road.
Closed: Christmas week.

How to get there: From Galway take N59 towards Clifden — 4 miles out. House signed on right.

Map Ref No: 11

48

Norman Villa

86 Lower Salthill
Galway
Co. Galway

Tel: 091-521131
Fax: 091-521131

Dee and Mark Keogh

It's not always easy to find a city address with a personal touch and a country house feeling, but Norman Villa manages both. This is down to Dee and Mark who have that ability to produce a friendly, chatty atmosphere from nothing. They seem to have time for all their guests and the general air of bonhomie spreads throughout — breakfast was conversational as well as delicious. The house itself was built in 1855 and you drive through a narrow tunnel to park securely in the courtyard where the old coachhouse used to be. To the rear of the building there are views over oak trees and a field, a nice glimpse of the open in the middle of busy Galway. Bedrooms aren't huge but subtly designed — again with a country feel. Lots of light during the day (none at night with light-tight shutters!), pine floors, brass beds and electric blankets, floral quilts, the odd exposed stone wall and high ceilings. The whole house is dotted with the Keoghs' modern Irish art collection. Let them advise you on what to do, where to eat, how to get there etc. They have maps and menus ready.

Rooms: 5: all doubles/triples with en suite shower.
Price: £32.50 p.p. Sing. supp. £7.
Breakfast: Included — full Irish.
Meals: Available in Galway.
Closed: Never!

How to get there: In Galway follow signs to Salthill, then Lower Salthill.

Map Ref No: 11

Clare Island Lighthouse

Clare Island
Westport
Co. Mayo

Tel: 098-45120
Fax: 098-45120
E-mail: clareislandlighthous@tinet.ie
www: http://homepage.tinet.ie/~clareislandlighthous

Monica and Robert Timmermans

As the mist lifts at primitive Roonagh passenger ferry, you see an imposing whitewashed lighthouse structure on the horizon, on the northern edge of Clare Island. The ferry moors up in the small island harbour where your transport is waiting. Passing dry stone walls, an old Landrover bumps along the unsurfaced road and makes its way up to the lighthouse. The light and keeper's cottages are perched 387 feet up on a cliff, like gannet's nests. The light was extinguished in 1965, the buildings abandoned to the elements for three decades. From 1992 to 1995 Robert and Monica restored and renovated the complex, making sure the romance of the place wasn't altered, only the levels of comfort. It is walkers rather than passing ships, who are encouraged by the warmth of the lights that glows through its windows today. All the rooms are fully centrally heated, the views are stunning and the welcome genuine. Monica lists the following things to do: *dolce farniente*, walking, hill-climbing, cliff-hiking, cycling, archaeological and island safaris, boat trips, island-hopping and sea-angling. Her table is unpretentious, based on local produce, fresh seafood and crustacean. An unforgettable experience.

Rooms: 5: all doubles with en suite bathrooms.
Price: £40 — £45 p.p.
Breakfast: Included — full Irish,
Meals: Dinner £20.
Closed: Never.

How to get there: From Westport go to Louisburgh and then to Roonagh Pier. Take the ferry from here (tel: 098-26307 or 25212 or 25045). You will be collected from Clare Island pier.

Map Ref No: 5

Rosturk Woods
Rosturk
Mulranny, Westport
Co. Mayo

Tel: 098-36264
Fax: 098-36264
E-mail: stoney@iol.ie

Louisa and Alan Stoney

This part of Mayo is not well known and yet it should be. Rosturk Woods is a modern house, completed in 1991, but it does not have the feel of something new. Its position is just wonderful. A long drive leads down through sparse woods and then you realize just how close to the sea you are. The huge kitchen, cluttered with the paraphernalia of cooking and children — mobiles, rugs, a small billiard table — leads out through double doors onto a long 'verandah' which looks straight onto Clew Bay and the island that you can walk to across hard sand at low tide. The bay harbours otters and a host of birdlife. This is a great place for those galvanised into action by the sea. Alan is a qualified sailing instructor and they organise boating and fishing, all with their own boats. Among the trees on their five acres there are a tennis court and a stream with three little waterfalls. The house can be self-catered or straight B&B — ask for more exact details when booking. Louisa is very natural and great fun and the house is veritably a family home — dogs, children... the lot. Ideal if you have kids yourself.

Rooms: 3 doubles/twins: 2 with en/s bathroom, 1 with en/s shower.
Price: £25 p.p. Sing. supp. £10.
Breakfast: Included — full Irish.
Meals: Dinner £20. Picnic lunches from £5.
Closed: December 1st — March 1st.

How to get there: From Newport take the Mulranny/Achill road for 7 miles — big blue sign for house on left.

Map Ref No: 5

Boheh Loughs Farmhouse

Liscarney   **Tel:** 098-21797
Westport
Co. Mayo

Aileen Large

At last a special place for Westport! And another for the lovely county of Mayo. Aileen and husband Frank (football fanatics may remember him? — he used to play for Chelsea and Northampton) have moved from England to set up this excellent-value B&B in a traditional lough-side Irish cottage. It seems tiny from the outside, although, Tardis-like, it's bigger inside. The renovation and extension of the original building have been sympathetic and the results are charming and cosy. Walls are washed in pretty colours with touches of gold here and there and the word 'sweet' keeps coming to mind. Sweet dining room with corner fireplace. Sweet bedrooms of doll's house proportions are found just inside the door which makes the house feel small. The family room is definitely the most appealing with its brass bed and patchwork quilt, and the twin is perfect for children. Showers are ordinary, but if you get a chance to poke your nose round the rest of the house grab it. It's all higgle and piggle, a bonsai gem of a house. Your very friendly hosts offer great value right by famous Croagh Patrick and the sea.

Rooms: 3: 1 double with en suite shower; 1 twin en suite shower; 1 family (double and a single) en/s shower.
Price: £17 p.p. Sing supp £4.
Breakfast: Included — full Irish.
Meals: Dinners for walkers by arrangement: £6 — £9. Vegetarians well catered for. Great restaurants in Westp't.
Closed: Christmas.

How to get there: Take N59 from Westport to Clifden. Approx 4 miles from Westport, set back from the road on right. Signed Boheh Loughs Farmhouse on road.

Map Ref No: 5   **52**

Enniscoe House

Castlehill
Nr Crossmolina, Ballina
Co. Mayo

Tel: 096-31112
Fax: 096-31773
E-mail: enniscoe@indigo.ie

Susan Kellett

In a self-deprecating moment Susan said of her lovely Georgian mansion: "Elegantly shabby is OK. Downright grotty is not." Would downright elegant be alright? In every way 'the last great house of Mayo' was one of my favourite places to stay. The house is set in parkland, with lawns and meadows rolling down to Lough Conn. There are five acres of Victorian pleasure garden, a network of unobtrusive trails through woods and fourteen fishing boats bobbing on the lake. This is a Heritage House of Ireland and some of its finest features are an oval landing, confusingly angled stairs, and a drawing room delicately described as 'fragile', ie full of antiques. Family portraits grace the walls — Susan descends from the original family who arrived in the area in the 1660s. As for the bedrooms: four-posters you need a ladder to get into, windows that stretch from floor to distant ceiling, antique dressers, Susan's mother's paintings, the view... and very cosy too. Nobody knows how Susan does all she does and remains such great company. Energy and brains, I expect. *Pets in the house by arrangement.*

Rooms: 6: 2 doubles with adjoining smaller bedrooms; 1 twin; 1 double; 2 doubles/twins: all with en suite bathrooms.
Price: £46 — £74 p.p. Sing. supp. £10. Special weekly and Dinner B&B rates available.
Breakfast: Included — full Irish.
Meals: Dinner £22. Packed lunches £6 — £8.
Closed: October 14th — April 1st (pre-booked groups in January).

How to get there: From Ballina take the N59 to Crossmolina. In Crossmolina turn left onto R315 (Castlebar Rd). House 2 miles out on left.

53

Map Ref No: 6

The Old Rectory

Easkey
Co. Sligo

Tel: 096-49181
Fax: 096-49181
E-mail: adlib@tinet.ie
www: http://homepage.tinet.ie/~forrestereaskey

Robert and Lorely Forrester

One of Ireland's many secrets, this area of Sligo/North Mayo remains fairly undiscovered by overseas visitors, although Easkey is firmly on any surfer's *mappa mundi*. The Old Rectory was built in the 1790s for its adjoining church and Lorely has brought her interior design creativity to bear so that each room today is a complete surprise; there are starry ceilings, gold curtains, pink walls with gold suns, wooden shutters; through bedroom windows you have views of the church, the river Easkey and even the sea. The whole property is surrounded by a high wall, enclosing lovely mature flower gardens where you come across bamboo and sub-tropical plants. Then there is the creeper-covered coach house where the Forresters run short courses, ranging from stone-wall-building to investing in the stock market; and the lovely stone courtyard where hurricane lamps hang, perfect for barbecues, jugs of Guinness, musical evenings. And everywhere there are animals — dogs, cats, sheep, lambs, hens. Lorely and Robert are a very friendly, easy-going young couple with much energy and creativity between them. Very reasonable prices too.

Rooms: 2: 1 double and 1 family sharing 1 bath and 1 shower.
Price: £22.50 p.p. Sing. supp. £8.
Breakfast: Included — full Irish.
Meals by arrangement: Supper en famille from £12.
Closed: Christmas.

How to get there: From Dublin to Sligo exit N4 dual carriageway at Coloooney and take old Sligo road to Ballisodare. L before bridge onto N59 to Ballina. Continue to Dromore West, turn R in village, signed Easkey 5 miles — Rectory next to church.

Map Ref No: 6

Temple House

Ballymote
Co. Sligo

Tel: 071-83329
Fax: 071-83808
E-mail: guests@templehouse.ie
www: http://www.templehouse.ie/

Deb and Sandy Perceval

Temple House is one of the most imposing and idiosyncratic places you're likely to stay anywhere in the world. Approached up a long parkland drive, passing the three ruins of previous Temple houses on your left, one medieval, one Tudor, one Jacobean, the great bulk of today's version (is it 100 rooms?) sits ponderously on higher ground looking down on the lake. The yawning outer and portrait-galleried inner halls evoke a glittering past of Far Eastern fortunes. Before a wonderful wild salmon supper take a glass of wine (they don't have a spirits licence) in a fireside sitting room where Deb ministers with engaging and reassuring ease. The bedrooms are to scale — one is called the half-acre room — and exude a rare air of a greater past. This feeling redoubles in the museum-like drawing room filled with wonderful Victoriana and still shaded by the gilt pelmetry, silk folds and gold braid ropes of the original curtains. The stunning lakeside parkland has the greenest grass and fattest lambs. Sandy grows all their vegetables organically (there is a massive walled garden) but is "allergic to perfumed products and sprays so please avoid". *Call for advice.*

Rooms: 5: 1 family suite with en suite bath; 1 double with en/s shower; 1 double with private sh; 1 twin en/s bath; 1 single en/s sh.
Price: £38 — £40 p.p. Sing. supp. £5.
Breakfast: Included — full Irish.
Meals: Dinner £19. Children's high tea (under 5) at 6.30 p.m.
Closed: November 30th — April 1st.

How to get there: From Sligo take N4 direction Dublin. Then N17 direction Galway. 0.25 miles past Ballinacarrow take left signed to Temple House.

55

Map Ref No: 6

Coopershill House

Riverstown
Co. Sligo

Tel: 071-65108
Fax: 071-65466
E-mail: ohara@coopershill.com

Brian and Lindy O'Hara

Coopershill is a fantastic place. From the moment you finally arrive, having wound up and around the long parkland drive, it never ceases to delight and amaze. In a house so handsome and greyly distinguished, you might expect a formal welcome but Brian waving gaily in his baggy cords and sweater could hardly be less so. You now assume the inside will be friendly dogs and worn old furniture. Not a bit of it — the stone-floored double entrance hall hung with flags and stags, white marble figurines in primrose alcoves and a fine 19th-century parchment wall map of Ireland might intimidate if not for their easy ways and the warm pot-bellied welcome of the stove. No pomp here but every care: "If a job's worth doing...," Brian says and every detail confirms that. Everything is exemplary. There are fresh flowers, beautiful pictures, a chaise longue in every room and amazing old beds with brand new mattresses. The king-sized bedroom on the top floor looks out over copper beeches and the River Unsin, but Brian and Lindy's favourite has a 4-poster and huge corner windows. The bathroom's pristine 1900 canopied bath, centred in its cool green-tiled grotto, will knock your socks off.

Rooms: 8: 1 twin, 5 doubles and 2 four-posters: all with en suite bathrooms except one with separate private bathroom.
Price: £50 — £57.50 p.p. Sing. supp. £10.
Breakfast: Included — full Irish.
Meals: Dinner £26.
Closed: November 1st — Mar 31st.

How to get there: From Sligo take N4 direction Dublin for 11 miles to Drumfin crossroads. Coopershill signed to left. Entrance is on left after 1.25 miles just before sharp turn.

Map Ref No: 6

Ross House

Ross
Riverstown
Co. Sligo

Tel: 071-65140

Oriel and Nicholas Hill-Wilkinson

When I first met Nicholas his overalls and face were smattered with mud as if to prove that, while some may merely *claim* to be working farmers, there was absolutely no doubting him. Both he and Oriel are infectious smilers, are obviously fascinated by others, love the variety guests afford them (the cheap and easy travelling they can do from their own sitting room)... and all in all seem to rejoice in life. Oriel promised herself she would only do one year of B&B. That was 20 years ago. "Last Wednesday we had one Tongan, one St Lucian and two Indians staying," said Nicholas with amazement in his voice. The 1890s farmhouse is Oriel's family home and is entered through a lovely flower-bedecked porch with flagstones outside. And all around there are cow fields and byres and the consequent sounds. Otherwise this is pure peace. Rooms are of varying sizes, in plain colours with modern furniture and brass beds — exactly what you would wish from down-to-earth farmhouse accommodation. Great for children. Nearby lies the archaeological site of Carrowkeel and its amazing passage tombs (which are a sort of tourist secret...).

Rooms: 6: 1 family with en suite shower; 1 double, 1 single and 2 family sharing 2 bathrooms; 1 twin with en suite shower.
Price: £20 — £22 p.p. Sing. supp. £3 dependent on season.
Breakfast: Included — full Irish.
Meals: Dinner £16. Packed lunches on request.
Closed: Never!

How to get there: From Sligo take N4 (Dublin Rd) for 8 miles to Drumfin. Left signed to Riverstown. Signs in village — house 1 mile out.

Map Ref No: 6

The Glebe House

Collooney
Co. Sligo

Tel: 071-67787
Fax: 071-30438
E-mail: glebehse@iol.ie

Brid and Marc Torrades

Brid and Marc have — almost famously — been long at restoring what was left of this old glebe house. I kept hearing about them from different parts of Ireland. The result is a country house full of personality — nothing remotely hotelly here, except perhaps the phones in bedrooms. The main event is the award-winning restaurant for which they are justly reknowned — finest local ingredients, fruit, veg and herbs from the old walled garden, an unusual selection of wines, seafood direct from Atlantic ports. And the atmosphere that goes with it is relaxed and rule-free — guests here really do unwind and make themselves at home. The main restaurant has painted wooden floors, red tablecloths, wood panelling, lovely wallpaper. Both this and the bistro are charming and informal. Country-style bedrooms are large with wooden beds, the odd sofa, magazines and views onto surrounding meadows. At the end of the garden the River Owenmore completes the rural tableau — it's good for canoeing or fishing. A perfect place to relax and enjoy excellent food in a home-from-home.

Rooms: 4: 2 double/twins with en suite bath; 1 double/twin with en/s shower; 1 double with en/s shower.
Price: £22.50 — £25 p.p. Sing. supp. £5.
Breakfast: Included — full Irish.
Meals: Restaurant dinners (5 courses) £22. A la carte also available. Summer bistro. Lunches for groups by arrangement.
Closed: 3 days at Christmas.

How to get there: From Sligo take N4 towards Dublin for 5 miles. First roundabout turn right, then first right again. Left after Quigleys Pub, then 400m (second) left up to the house (signed).

Map Ref No: 6

Markree Castle

Collooney
Co. Sligo

Tel: 071-67800
Fax: 071-67840
E-mail: markree@iol.ie

Charles and Mary Cooper

There is quite a story to how Charles ended up back in the family castle after it had lain empty for 36 years. 15 generations of Coopers are in the hall's stained-glass family tree and five more since the glazier stopped work. The fantastic Victorian Gothic detail was added later, but the 15th-century heart remains. Charles and Mary started out seven years ago with three bedrooms and have now inventively reclaimed 30 — some high up and split-levelled in a surreal roofscape of lead, buttressed chimneys and crenellations. Others, vaulted and panelled with exotic woods, look out through arched and mullioned windows. There is an extravagance of features: galleries, long luxuriously carpeted passageways, deep carved panelling and angel corbels hanging from a soaring atrium ceiling. The dining room is a rococo feast of heavily-ornamented plaster, gilt cherubs and mirrors. The cosy lounge is a mere 23 yards long and the fireplaces hold vast smouldering chunks of wood. Charles, the boyish-looking chap casually dressed at the reception computer, eschews formality, rules or signs. The result is a remarkable, familiar ease. The park is beautiful and the river runs close by.

Rooms: 30: twins, doubles etc: all with en suite bathrooms.
Price: £48 — £55 p.p. Sing. supp. £12.
Breakfast: Included — full Irish.
Meals: Dinner £23 or £26. Light lunches and Sunday lunch £13.50.
Closed: December 24th — 26th.

How to get there: From Sligo take N4 direction Dublin for 7 miles. Turn left at first roundabout and entrance at top of hill on right. 1 mile avenue to castle.

Map Ref No: 6

Ardtarmon House

Ballinfull
Co. Sligo

Tel: 071-63156
Fax: 071-63156

Charles and Christa Henry

What a setting. Surrounded by its labyrinth of walls and outbuildings, one a thatched self-catering cottage, from Ardtarmon's top-floor parapets you can see it all: the sea, the Mayo Mountains, Knocknarea mountain by Sligo airport and the Yeats country mountains over in Leitrim. It's only a three-minute stroll through the woods, down a lane and across a field and you have your own private beach — well, nobody who isn't staying is likely to find it anyway, so secluded is this! The gardens and orchards that surround are old and verdant at the moment (if you know what I mean) but are next on Charles and Christa's long list of 'what to do'. That's how I like gardens anyway. They are such a nice couple (with a young family) and are new to B&B. Relaxed and quick to laughter, they ensure the atmosphere is wonderfully hospitable. Charles does the cooking, solid country-style Irish, and points you off on walks to build your appetite. The guest rooms upstairs are newly decorated, lots of space, huge beds, fluffy pillows and duvets you sink into, new carpets everywhere and views of the garden. A great new place to discover.

Rooms: 4: 1 double with en suite bath; 2 doubles with en suite shower; 1 double and single with en/s shower.
Price: £25 — £30 p.p. Sing. supp. £5.
Breakfast: Included — full Irish.
Meals: Dinner £15.
Closed: December 19th — January 3rd.

How to get there: From Sligo take N15 north towards Donegal for 5 miles to Drumcliffe. Turn L towards Carney — 1 mile. In village take signs to Raghley for 4.5 miles, L at Dunleavy's shop. 1.5 miles gate lodge and drive on L.

The North Midlands

Rockwood House

Cloverhill
Belturbet
Co. Cavan

Tel: 047-55351
Fax: 047-55373
E-mail: jbmac@tinet.ie

Susan and Jim McCauley

I arrived at Rockwood as usual in bright sunshine (and an hour late). A peaceful scene this brand new house, surrounded by trees and garden in a very untouristy slice of Ireland. There is a wooden gate that leads off the garden into the next-door wood, abode of red squirrels and pine martins which are regularly sighted. I was greeted by an enthusiastic westie (that's a dog) and sat and drank a relaxed coffee with Susan and Jim on the sunlit patio. It can't always be like this and in colder weather the house becomes very cosy with real fires. They clearly enjoy entertaining, are good at it and suited to it. They have designed the house as they wanted, one of the great advantages of building your own. Immaculate guest rooms have carpeted floors, are painted in pastel colours (blue, yellow) and everything is brand new. Room to move around in, lack of clutter and lots of well-appreciated extras such as little shampoo bottles. This is very much a B&B so don't expect mod cons like phones in the rooms. Good value in a very friendly home.

Rooms: 4: 1 double and 3 twins with en suite shower. 1 extra bathroom.
Price: £19 p.p. No sing. supp.
Breakfast: Included — full Irish.
Meals: The Olde Post Inn restaurant in the village.
Closed: One week at Christmas.

How to get there: From Cavan follow signs for Monaghan for 4 miles to Butlersbridge; bear right in Butlersbridge. House 2 miles on left-hand side.

Map Ref No: 8

Hollywell

Liberty Hill
Carrick-on-Shannon
Co. Leitrim

Tel: 078-21124
Fax: 078-21124

Rosaleen and Tom Maher

It was Rosaleen and Tom who used to run the big hotel in the town here. Now they have time to pay individual attention again and are far happier for it. This house is brim-full of flair and vibrancy. Arise from under your white, delicately-embroidered duvet and crisp sheets. Throw back the shutters upstairs in your brass twin or draped queen and gaze at the river. Look down and, watching their slow progress through the wide reed-banked course, imagine yourself upon one of the riverboats plying the Shannon-Lough Erne waterway. This is the beauty of Hollywell; it has turned its back on the town, thanks to a driveway that's something of a magic wardrobe. You are in Carrick — a busy market town — you've been at the Oarsman 'til closing (great bar food and craic in an old beer-soaked wooden interior) and returned 100 yards across the bridge and left up the drive. The town disappears, the bustle is a memory. Any time now it'll be time for breakfast. And it was no coincidence that next morning I found my place laid at the burr walnut table which I'd particularly admired the night before.

Rooms: 4: 1 family and 2 doubles with en suite bathrooms; 1 twin with en suite shower.
Price: £28 — £35 p.p. Sing. supp. £5 — £10.
Breakfast: Included — full Irish.
Meals: Not available.
Closed: December 20th — January 2nd.

How to get there: From N4 (Dublin — Sligo Rd) on Carrick side of Shannon. Cross bridge and take first left turn up lane past Ging's Pub. Hollywell just after pub up driveway on left.

Map Ref No: 7

Clonalis House

Castlerea
Co. Roscommon

Tel: 0907-20014
Fax: 0907-20014

Pyers and Marguerite O'Conor Nash

Approached up a mile-long drive, Clonalis sits aloof in its 700 acres, 250 of which are wood and parkland. Marguerite and Pyers have worked hard on the grounds and have now opened up old woodland walks... not prettified but rough. There are two (brown trout) rivers on the property and a walled garden. This is a special house, not least for the wealth of O'Conor history that runs through the building like a supporting wall. Pyers is the expert here. It was built in 1878 by Charles Owen O'Conor Don in the Victorian Italianate style with 45 rooms, but the family has been on this land for an estimated 1500 years. Its history is fully Irish, a rarity amongst houses of this stature. One of the highlights of the ground floor where all is grand is the wonderful library. The bedrooms are impressive, a four-poster here, a half-tester there, gilt-framed mirrors, elegant fireplaces, massive bathrooms, all full of old family furniture and looking out over a wonderful array of copper beeches. Pyers and Marguerite are hugely energetic and welcoming and food is of high repute.

Rooms: 4: 3 doubles and 1 twin: all with en suite bathrooms, but one double has a separate loo.
Price: £42 — £49.50 p.p. Sing. supp. £6. NB 10% discount for 3 or more nights.
Breakfast: Included — full Irish.
Meals: Dinner £22.50 (with 24 hours notice). Packed lunches on request.
Closed: October 1st — mid-April.

How to get there: From Athlone take Roscommon Rd off bypass, circle north round Roscommon Town on bypass, left signed to Castlerea. Clonalis House well signposted in town.

Map Ref No: 6

The Old Rectory

Ardcarne
Boyle
Co. Roscommon

Tel: 079-67149

Bernie and Jim Reynolds

Jim and Bernie are an exceptionally friendly young couple with three small boys, so the atmosphere at the Old Rectory is charged with energy. Bernie seems to do everything at once without fuss — I think she may have baked those cakes while we were talking — and the first thing you notice about her is her obvious enjoyment of other people. Outside, roaming among the ruined outbuildings and over the lawn, are roosters, hens, ducks, Samson the cat and a pony that slowly mows the buttercupped field in front of the house — great for kids. Down the road is the Lough Key Forest National Park. Adults looking for exercise should consult Jim who's mad on hill-walking — not something you might think of in an area more famous for its lakes, but it's not far to the Arigna Mountains. The house is decorated in plain colours with pretty bedrooms, wooden floors, huge zip-and-link beds, pot plants, nice timber-framed windows looking onto the meadowy paddock... and downstairs there's an amazing bathroom with wooden posts, and miniature bottles crowding the shelves. This is real down-to-earth, Irish country hospitality at its best.

Rooms: 3: 1 double, 1 family with en suite; 1 double with private bathroom.
Price: £18.50 p.p.
Breakfast: Included — full Irish/Continental.
Meals: Available locally.
Closed: Christmas .

How to get there: Take N4 west out of Carrick-on-Shannon. Turn right at Knockvicar/Keadue road. First house on left, beside the Ardcarne Garden Centre.

Map Ref No: 7

Glencarne House

Carrick-on-Shannon
Co. Roscommon

Tel: 079-67013

Agnes Harrington

Agnes has been doing B&B for 28 years and still loves it! She is one of the few for whom the comfort, welcome and environment she provides for her many oft-returning guests is of paramount importance. She is always there to greet you. No detail is overlooked — flowers are fresh, butter is curled on a plate, all her ingredients are completely farm-fresh, breakfast is a feast, open fires are laid... and the house is a dangerous place for dust and dirt. Sitting on a hill the house looks down over fields from the front and is surrounded on its other flanks by a tangly garden and its 100-acre farm. Although carpets are a bit bold on occasion, bedrooms are very comfortable with plain-coloured walls, warm rugs, brass beds, lovely wooden windows — and there is lots of light. Carrick-on-Shannon sits on 40 lakes, a major attraction for boaters and fisherpeople. And opposite Glencarne House lies the Lough Key forest park with its walks and bog gardens. You will be very well looked after by Agnes and her food is all home-cooked.

Rooms: 4: 2 doubles/twins with en suite shower; 1 double with en suite bath; 1 twin with en suite shower.
Price: £22 p.p. Sing. supp. £5.
Breakfast: Included — full Irish.
Meals: Dinner £17.
Closed: Nov 1st — March 1st.

How to get there: From Dublin take N4 towards Sligo (100 miles), past Carrick-on-Shannon, 4.5 miles, house signed on left up drive (0.5 miles past golf club).

Map Ref No: 7

Glebe House

Rathowen
Co. Westmeath

Tel: 043-76189
Fax: 043-76172
E-mail: cmagan@tinet.ie

Catherine Magan

Some mention must be made of Catherine's home-made breads, pâté and quiche, so I thought I'd start with that. I found it really difficult to stop eating and this was meant to be a mid-afternoon snack. She cooks everything herself and dinners are special. The house itself is large, secluded and Georgian, swathed in Russian and Virginia creepers with a grass tennis court at the front. There are many fine original Georgian features as well as the odd curiosity such as the drawing room shutters that disappear yards into the ground. The Magans (he's a doctor in Mullingar) have recently done the place up in bold colours and with great comfort in mind. The bedrooms are large with wood floors and rugs, hearths, powerful showers, big towels, and views onto the walled orchard with its pears, cherries and roses. One room has a solid four-poster, one bathroom a painted ivy mural with a great deep bath. The house does not suffer as some big Irish houses do from the cold, thanks to good insulation from double-glazing. Catherine has only just started having guests and is greatly enthusiastic about it.

Rooms: 4: 3 doubles and 1 double/twin, 2 with en suite bath, 2 with en suite shower.
Price: £28.50 — £36 p.p. Sing. supp. £6.
Breakfast: Included — full Irish.
Meals: Dinner £20. Packed lunches and lunches also by request.
Closed: Christmas week.

How to get there: From Mullingar take N4 towards Longford for 12 miles, immediately as you enter Rathowen turn left and follow past the school to the end (150 yds).

Map Ref No: 7

Lough Owel Lodge

Cullion
Nr Mullingar
Co. Westmeath

Tel: 044-48714
Fax: 044-48771
E-mail: aginnell@hotes.iol.com
www: www.anglefire.com/fx/aginnell

Martin and Aideen Ginnell

Come screaming down the N4, remember to turn left and suddenly, as is so often the case in Ireland, you're in the middle of deep countryside. Lough Owel Lodge is a modern house that has been added to since the 1940s and the design has paid, unsurprisingly, close attention to the view. The open-plan sitting-dining room has full-wall, wood-framed windows that look down over Lough Owel, sheep fields, the tennis court and beyond to writer J.P. Donleavy's property. The Ginnells' land goes down to the lake (it's a 10 minute walk) and trout fishing can be arranged with ghillies and boats. There is literally nothing that spoils this view for miles. Aideen and Martin are naturally friendly and incorporate guests easily into their bustling family home. Dinners (all together unless discretion forbids it) are taken round a lovely old inherited dining table. If 'doing' is what you're about they have books all over the place and the Fore Trail crosses this 'Land of Lake and Legend'. Rooms have some lovely beds — a four-poster and a 150-year-old half-tester — and all the bedrooms are unusual shapes. Great for children.

Rooms: 5: 1 family suite with en suite bath; 1 twin, 2 four-posters and 1 double with en suite showers.
Price: £19 — £21 p.p. Sing. supp. £6.
Breakfast: Included — full Irish.
Meals: Dinner £14. Packed lunches £4.50.
Closed: December 1st — March 17th.

How to get there: From Mullingar follow signs, onto the N4 towards Sligo. House signed left by the lake.

Mornington House

Mornington
Multyfarnham near Mullingar
Co. Westmeath

Tel: 044-72191
Fax: 044-72338
E-mail: morning@indigo.ie
www: http://www.indigo.ie/morning

Anne and Warwick O'Hara

Seclusion here is absolute. With the shutters closed on your bedroom windows you could sleep all day... providing the odd distant rogue cuckoo or the chimney jackdaws sleep too. You approach Mornington through thick trees — the manifold guardians of the property that seem to hem it in on all sides — and follow the drive round, past fields. The central section was built in 1710, the front in 1897 and the wing in 1906, a combination of effort by the founders, the Daly Family and the original O'Haras who took up residence in 1858. Some bedrooms are large, in bright colours, with proper bathrooms, oval baths, brass beds and views that include the wonderful solitary oak tree that stands like a general surveying his troops. The field of battle stretches behind and disappears over a hill. There's a lake out there too. Downstairs, carpets fade as they approach long ranks of park-facing windows. And presiding over all this are Warwick and Anne, returned from 11 years in Canada, who are genuinely dedicated hosts and produce the most delicious meals. I devoured those breakfast pancakes. *Children by arrangement.*

Rooms: 5: 3 doubles, 1 single and 1 twin: all with private facilities (2 en suite).
Price: £35 p.p. Sing. supp. £5. 3 days including dinner for £159 p.p.
Breakfast: Included — full Irish.
Meals: Dinner £22.50.
Closed: November 2nd — April 3rd.

How to get there: From N4/Mullingar bypass take R394 for 8 km towards Castlepollard. Left at Wood Pub in Crookedwood, then 2 km to first junction. Turn right, house 1 mile on right.

Map Ref No: 7

Mearescourt House

Rathconrath
Mullingar
Co. Westmeath

Tel: 044-55112
Fax: 044-55112

Brendan and Eithne Pendred

Approach Mearescourt up a lovely drive, escorted by an avenue of trees, to this large Georgian mansion and spend a moment taking in the wonderful setting. The house sits in 350 acres of park, farm and woodland — and the grass extends, awash with buttercups and dotted with magnificent horse chestnuts, from the front of the house. To the right lies the rejuvenated 18th-century lake. Rooms at the back, such as the smaller sitting room, a cosier room for the winter than the huge, high-ceilinged drawing room, look over the walled garden, all set about with monkey-puzzle trees. Upstairs bedrooms are huge, with brass beds and plain bright walls, bay windows and, naturally, mellifluous views. Eithne and Brendan are an easy-going, gentle couple who offer a family home environment. They didn't even like the idea of leaving brochures on the hall table for fear of introducing a hotelly feel until constant requests finally made them succumb — but it is still a house blessedly free of TV. This is a green leafy country area in the sleepy Midlands where you will find absolute seclusion. Great value.

Rooms: 6: 2 family, 2 doubles and 1 twin/double with en suite bathrooms; 1 twin with own bathroom.
Price: £25 — £27 p.p. Sing. supp. £10.
Breakfast: Included — full Irish.
Meals: Dinner £18.
Closed: Christmas week.

How to get there: From Mullingar take Ballymahon Rd for 5 or 6 miles through Rathconrath. 2 miles past village at bottom of steep hill turn right, then first left (signed). House on right up drive.

Map Ref No: 7

Crookedwood House

Crookedwood
Mullingar
Co. Westmeath

Tel: 044-72165
Fax: 044-72166
E-mail: cwoodhse@iol.ie

Noel and Julie Kenny

Come to this hideaway in the Midlands for all your creature comforts. Of the original house built in 1774, only the basement restaurant survives today since Noel and Julie redesigned the place to their own specifications. A series of rooms, all with very good quality solid modern furniture and mod cons, are laid out as in a small hotel. And this *is* a small hotel, only eight rooms, and the personal touch is definitely there. You see as much of Noel as he can spare, but really his realm is the kitchen downstairs and Julie takes care of the pastoral side of the business with great charm. It is the basement restaurant that really pulls in the customers, though, and rightly. The house sits on top of a hill and has really lovely views of lakes and hills — surprising for this part of Ireland, it's usually more rolling than this. Go for a walk, or perhaps a spot of fishing on Lough Derravaragh, come back for a real bath, and then make your way down to the cosy wooden bar before a gas fire for a drink... and the agony of making a final decision with the menu. Meals are heavenly.

Rooms: 8: all doubles/twins with en suite bathrooms.
Price: £40 — £50 p.p. Sing. supp. £10.
Breakfast: Included — full Irish.
Meals: Dinner £25, Sunday lunches £14.50.
Closed: January (2 weeks) and all bank holidays.

How to get there: From Dublin take 3rd exit on Mullingar bypass (signed to Castlepollard). Drive to Crookedwood village. Turn right at Wood Pub. Continue 1.5 miles to house.

Map Ref No: 8

Reynella House

Bracklyn
Mullingar
Co. Westmeath

Tel: 044-64137

Margaret and Pat Lynch

Reynella is a charming 18th-century Georgian house built by its original English landlord, Richard Reynell. Squarely set at the top of its drive, it is fronted by a swan lake and fields and at the back are wonderful, high-walled gardens and a walled paddock with an arched gate. Birds love it here. The farm itself stretches back up the lanes where there are 65 acres of mixed forestry, so woodland walks abound. Inside, there are lovely original touches to the house, with its wooden floors, arched door-frames and lovely cupola-lit staircase. The rooms are huge and simply furnished. For these prices you would be pressed to find more impressive rooms, with big comfortable beds and lovely lake views. They have huge bathrooms, too, with chess-board pattern tiles and one has a free-standing bath. Margaret and Patrick are very friendly and will help visitors as much as possible, whether it be about the house or handing out information on fishing the nearby lakes. It is all excellent value. *Self-catering cottages from £175 — £250 per week.*

Rooms: 3: 1 double, 1 double/twin and 1 family; 2 with en suite bath and shower, 1 with en suite shower.
Price: £17 p.p. Sing. supp. £4.
Breakfast: Included — full Irish.
Meals: Available in Mullingar & Delvin.
Closed: Never!

How to get there: From Mullingar take the N52 towards Delvin for 8 miles. House signed on main road to right up a drive.

Temple Country House and Spa

Horseleap
Moate
Co. Westmeath

Tel: 0506-35118
Fax: 0506-35008
E-mail: templespa@spiders.ie
www: http://www.spiders.ie/templespa

Bernadette and Declan Fagan

The idea here is to provide relaxing breaks away from the in-tray-out-tray influence of the outside world, to smooth out those knots in the neck that have built up in front of the computer. Guests are *not* encouraged to jump in their cars at seven every morning to charge round significant chunks of Ireland and return exhausted just in time for dinner. Take one of the house bikes instead, or even walk! Temple provides massages, places to read or think... or not think. And now they have added a relaxation annexe complete with sauna, steam room, massage rooms and — the jewel in the crown! — a miraculous hydrotherapy bath. It's a lovely old house (200 years) with surprisingly large bedrooms, big brass beds, proper bathrooms, thick carpets and views over lawns and fields. Guests eat excellent food together in an atmospheric, candelit dining room. Declan (an English language teacher) and Bernadette, a self-trained cook, dedicate themselves to helping people de-stress; their easy-going hospitality influences the mood of the whole place — great for kids and those who have grown weary of the city.

Rooms: 8: 2 doubles/twins en/s bath; 2 doubles en/s bath; 1 family en/s bath; 3 twins en/s bath; 1 single en/s.
Price: £35 — £40 p.p. Sing. supp. £10. Inclusive weekend and midweek spa programmes available.
Breakfast: Included — full Irish.
Meals: Dinner £18. Packed lunches on request.
Closed: December 1st — February 1st.

How to get there: From Moate take N6 towards Dublin for 4 miles. Turn left (signed). House 0.5 miles further on left.

Map Ref No: 12

Louth
•
Meath
•
Monaghan
•

North of Dublin

Red House
Ardee
Co. Louth

Tel: 041-53523

Linda Connolly and Fred Bereen

On a hot summer's day I can think of few places I'd rather be. Lie out in the walled garden by the tennis court and sheep paddocks, cool off in the pool. Red House is a Georgian oasis surrounded by 40 acres of woodland and garden and, whatever the attractions of nearby Newgrange and the Boyne Valley, it would be hard to dislodge me from my new home. The house was built in about 1800 by the Fortescues and the bedrooms are particularly special. Mine was *massive*, with windows requiring several hinges on their shutters and, although there were two armchairs, a round table, a huge chest of drawers, a full-length mirror, a wardrobe and a dressing table in there with me, there were still acres of thick carpet for me to roam. The bathroom was nearly as big. Linda seems to look after you without putting herself out and you feel at home almost immediately. Meals are taken together unless otherwise requested. The long dining table can seat two at each end which allows a certain amount of privacy (probably more than the average restaurant!) and there is a smaller table in the bay window. *Ask about children.*

Rooms: 3: 1 twin with private bathroom; 1 double with en suite bathroom; 1 double/twin with private bathroom.
Price: £35 — £45 p.p. Sing. supp. £10.
Breakfast: Included — full Irish.
Meals: Dinner £22.50.
Closed: December 20th — January 15th.

How to get there: From Dublin take N2 towards Ardee. In Ardee turn right onto N52 — 0.5 miles, house on left.

Map Ref No: 8

Ghan House

Carlingford
Co. Louth

Tel: 042-937-3682
Fax: 042-937-3682
E-mail: ghanhouse@tinet.ie

Paul, Cairlinn and Joyce Carroll

Pure serendipity led me to Ghan House (I was looking for somewhere else that turned out to have closed its doors). Some first-time guests were lunching outside this early 18th-century house when I drove up. Rarely have I met such enthusiasm; I got quite caught up in it. Carlingford itself is Ireland's most lovely medieval town, with abbey and castle; it's right on the coast and Ghan House is enclosed within the ancient walls. To the front the house looks across the lough to the Mournes. Behind lie the herb garden, a churchyard and Slieve Foy. The herb garden comes in handy for the cookery school that is run from the basement. Dinners (and everything you eat!) are special. There are arched doorways, corbelled ceilings, a half-tester bed, proper bathrooms... and lots to do. Paul's sister runs the riding centre and all manner of aquatic activities are available, too. The Carrolls are very friendly (I was introduced to everyone) and whether you prefer sitting by a fire, reading, or turning your hand to fishing / archery / windsurfing / sailing / golf — all available locally — it will be great fun.

Rooms: 4: 1 double with en suite bath; 2 doubles/twins with en suite bath; 1 single with en suite shower.
Price: £25 — £45 p.p. Sing. supp. £10.
Breakfast: Included — full Irish.
Meals: Dinners should be booked in advance: from £15. Rest'nt open Sat-Sun — booking recommended.
Closed: Christmas.

How to get there: Take N1 north from Dublin for 53 miles. Turn right just after Dundalk at main roundabout signed to Carlingford. 15 minute drive, house signed on left as you enter village on main road.

Map Ref No: 9

74

Boltown House

Kells
Co. Meath

Tel: 046-43605

Jean and Susan Wilson

Boltown was built as a farmhouse in the 1740-60s and it's still one now, much loved by its present owner, Jean. Its marble fireplaces, thick faded rugs and creaking floorboards all speak of times past. Jean loves having people to stay and is terrifically good at it. The attempt to find her was one of my less exalted feats of orienteering, but each time I wound down the window to ask the way it was clear everyone knew her and everyone liked her enormously. (The Irish are better at liking people than giving directions!) The house stands secluded among cow fields and there's a lovely horse chestnut in the garden that bears its load of rooks with good grace. The staircase splits to a double landing with concave ceiling upstairs and the three charming bedrooms lie off it. They are big, old-fashioned with sweet wooden windows and shutters, deep baths and views of the garden. Susan's dinners are delicious, using the freshest ingredients, concentrating on quality rather than elaboration. You are well away from the main tourist areas here and life has a slow rural hum.

Rooms: 3: 2 doubles with en suite bathroom; 1 double with private bathroom.
Price: £28 p.p. No sing. supp.
Breakfast: Included — full Irish.
Meals: Dinner £24.
Closed: Christmas week.

How to get there: From Kells take the Oldcastle Rd out of town. 4 miles, past petrol station, 2nd left, house 0.75 miles on right. Not signed. It's the first 2-storey house with a short drive on the right.

Map Ref No: 8

Lennoxbrook

Kells (Ceanannas Mor)
Co. Meath

Tel: 046-45902

Pauline Mullan

You enter the grounds through a full and low tunnel of foliage. The 18th-century house is sheltered from the main road by trees and a stream that Pauline struggles to keep visible through vigorously regenerative undergrowth. The house itself has an old-style feel to it, with the odd creaking stair, wooden slatted ceilings, wooden floors, oak furniture and proper bathrooms that are not necessarily adjoining. Pauline has a real feeling for old houses and shuns the idea of breaking up this fine house to suit modern conformists. There are low, narrow doorways that lead to bedrooms, some with bay windows — and there is one lovely bathroom down three steps with an original turn-of-the-century bath, a room festooned with green plant life. This is a living family house — Pauline's three daughters, Louise, Sally and Anna, are all at home and as helpful as their respective ages allow — and Pauline herself is great fun, enormously relaxed and a mine of local information on historic Kells and its megalithic heritage. Meals are taken communally and I found myself still drinking port with my Australian co-diners at one o'clock in the morning.

Rooms: 4: 1 triple and 1 twin sharing 2 bathrooms; 2 doubles with en suite showers.
Price: £16 — £20 p.p. Sing. supp. £5.
Breakfast: Included — full Irish.
Meals: Dinner £12. Packed lunches on request.
Closed: Christmas.

How to get there: From Kells take N3 towards Cavan — 3 miles outside Kells house signed on right after Burmah petrol station.

Map Ref No: 8

76

Mountainstown House

Castletown-Kilpatrick   **Tel:** 046-54154/54195
Navan   **Fax:** 046-54154
Co. Meath

John and Diana Pollock

Mountainstown is a Dutch Wren and early Georgian house and generations of Pollocks have been there since 1796. The fields in front of the house teem with horses, cows and donkeys and everywhere guinea fowl, peacocks, turkeys, geese and dogs range free. Inside, huge grand rooms lead one to another, servants' corridors running obediently along behind the scenes. All the original pine floors have recently been sanded and the huge bay windows and massive mirrors give the whole house a bright, airy, gleaming feel. There is a lovely drawing room with coral wallpaper and large bay windows with grand curtain rail and curtains. The bedrooms are spectacular. Some, with wooden floors, are enormous, one with an antique four-poster; but it is the windows which really make the rooms special, running from floor to ceiling so that the lovely views are visible from everywhere and light floods in. Surrounded by its 800 acres of farmland and parkland, Mountainstown is presided over by the breathlessly busy Diana, who welcomes guests with enormous friendliness and energy.

Rooms: 5: 3 doubles with en suite bathrooms; 1 double and 1 single sharing 1 bathroom.
Price: £25 — £55 p.p. Sing. supp. 10%. Children 1-10 in cots or camp-beds £10. Babies free.
Breakfast: Included — full Irish.
Meals: Dinners £20, with 24 hours notice.
Closed: December 22nd — January 3rd.

How to get there: From Navan take Kingscourt Rd for 7 miles, through Wilkinstown, first L after Burmah garage on R-hand side (there are two!). Follow for 1 mile to church. Turn R, house 200yds on L (signed to Mountainstown Stud). Black iron gate.

Map Ref No: 8

Killyon

Dublin Rd
Navan
Co. Meath

Tel: 046-71224
Fax: 046-72766

Michael and Sheila Fogarty

You might think Killyon slightly unprepossessing on arrival, a modern house right on the Navan — Dublin road. But I suggest you park and go in for what would have been a complete surprise if I hadn't already ruined it. The other side of the house looks straight onto the Boyne River from an elevated position and the verandah/balcony is a wonderful place to have breakfast on a sunny day. The breakfast is something they specialise in and everything is made by Sheila, including the yoghurt. On the other side of the river lies a park which means their view is safe. The river is home to a host of wildlife including swans, otters, foxes, kingfishers and all manner of birdlife. Walk along the tow-path to old castles and ruins and find a sheltered unspoilt, untouristy spot for a picnic. The water is crystal clear and great for swimming and fish-spotting. The house is deceptively large with four floors, cool in summer, very warm in winter and double-glazing ensures quiet from the road. Sheila and Michael are an unpretentious, easy-going couple and insist there are no rules or regulations. They merely ask their guests to lay back and float downstream.

Rooms: 4: 3 doubles and 1 triple; 2 with en suite bath, 2 with en suite shower.
Price: £20 — £25 p.p. Sing supp. £5.
Breakfast: Included — full Irish.
Meals: Dinner £14 (with 24 hrs notice). Excellent restaurants in Navan.
Closed: Christmas Eve and Day.

How to get there: From Dublin take N3 north for 25 miles. As you enter Navan (river on your right) the house is on the main road opposite Ardboyne Hotel.

Map Ref No: 8

78

Annesbrook

Duleek
Co. Meath

Tel: 041-23293
Fax: 041-23024

Kate Sweetman

Kate finds it easier to be an easy-going and charming hostess than a businesswoman, and Annesbrook is a haven on the busy east coast. There is an incredible stillness about the place. You enter through a narrow gatehouse known as 'the pockets' locally, because the two sides look like pockets if you're into comparing things to trousers. Up a leafy drive, then, to confront this large, slightly eccentric house which has grown organically since the 1700s. It is basically two main rooms downstairs — nicely proportioned dining and drawing rooms with soft sofas and a lovely carved marble fireplace, gilt mirror and yellow plasterwork — and bedrooms upstairs. This didn't stop me getting lost in the arched doorways and passages. Beds are enormous but all the rooms have a peaceful, uncluttered feeling of space, some looking onto a courtyard where cottages surround a folly. The modern paintings that crowd the walls downstairs are by Kate's daughter and an artist who resides somewhere about the property. Everyone sits at the same table for dinner. Come and switch off for a few days.

Rooms: 5: 2 family and 1 twin with en suite bath; 1 double and 1 twin with en suite shower.
Price: £30 — £35 p.p. Sing. supp. £8. Reductions for more than 1 night.
Breakfast: Included — full Irish.
Meals: Dinner £18 (book by 11.30 a.m. same day).
Closed: October 1st — May 1st.

How to get there: From Dublin take N2 towards Derry through Ashbourne; 4.5 miles later turn right signed Drogheda/Duleek. Annesbrook 4.5 miles on that road (R152) on the left.

Map Ref No: 8

The Old Workhouse
Dunshaughlin
Co. Meath

Tel: 01-8259251
Fax: 01-8259251
E-mail: comfort@a-vip.com

Niamh Colgan

The Old Workhouse was another one of those places I seemed to hear about all the time before my visit; it was clear that the ambience had greatly changed for the better since its 19th-century origins. Later there were 500 Belgian refugees here. Today it is a refuge from other forms of strife. Niamh (pronounced Neeve) does all the work and the huge amounts of care and attention she puts in ensure that guests come back. She's a wizard in the kitchen too and was being checked out while I was there by the Meath Society for Good Food... a sort of gastronomic police force; another (more regular) guest told me dinner was wonderful every night... and Niamh holds the prize for the "Best Breakfast in Ireland" too. Upstairs there is a huge drawing room with dark blue walls, wooden beams and an open fire (Niamh lights fires wherever you go); the room has a dark, cool feeling and if more than six sit down to dinner that's where you eat. Rooms are very comfortable, with pressure showers, a sherry decanter, bowls of fruit and sweets. When you come up from dinner you will find someone has closed the blinds and folded back the bed. I wonder who.

Rooms: 4: 1 double/twin with en suite bath and shower; 1 double with own bath and sh; 1 d/twin with en/s shower; 1 double with en/s sh.
Price: £30 — £40 p.p. Sing. supp. £10 — £15.
Breakfast: Included — full Irish and buffet.
Meals: Dinner £25 minimum 6 people (available from October to May inclusive).
Closed: One week at Christmas.

How to get there: From Dublin take N3 north towards Navan for 16 miles. House on right on main road, 1 mile before Dunshaughlin. 20 minutes from airport and Dublin City.

Map Ref No: 13

80

Hilton Park

Clones
Co. Monaghan

Tel: 047-56007
Fax: 047-56033
E-mail: hiltonpk@indigo.ie
www: http://www.tempoweb.com/hilton/

Johnny and Lucy Madden

Hilton Park could be a tourist attraction in its own right. It is one of Ireland's most imposing country houses and guests are lucky on all counts. Built by Johnny's ancestor in 1734, it was remodelled in the Italianate manner in the 1870s. Put your bags down (or get Johnny to — I wasn't allowed to carry mine) by your huge, high four-poster and take in the original wallpaper, the *chaise longue*, the view across lawns to the lake. The adjoining bathroom is so vast that once immersed in the free-standing bath — in the exact centre of the room — you feel as though you've been cast adrift in a boat. Go for a stroll down by the lake, enclosed by banks of tall trees and rhododendron, with its gravel walkways and jetty, swans and fish. Dinners are memorable too. Guests sit down all together or separately, as they choose, their faces lit by a large open fire while dark wood panelling and candles create a cosy, intimate atmosphere despite the size of the room. Every ingredient is as fresh as possible, picked minutes before cooking from the garden. Breakfast is taken in floods of morning light. A special place indeed. *Children over 7 welcome.*

Rooms: 6: 3 doubles; 2 family; 1 twin: all with en suite bathrooms.
Price: £57.50 — £67.50 p.p. Sing. supp. £10.
Breakfast: Included — full Irish.
Meals: Dinner £25 (wines from £13.50).
Closed: October 1st — March 31st (except for groups).

How to get there: From Cavan take Clones Rd then fork right at Statoil petrol station for Ballyhaise. Through Ballyhaise and Scotshouse; after 2.5 miles take first entrance on left after Clones golf club.

Map Ref No: 8

Glynch House

Newbliss
Clones
Co. Monaghan

Tel: 047-54045
Fax: 047-54321
E-mail: mirth@tinet.ie
www: http://homepage.tinet.ie/~glynchfarmhouse.

Martha O'Grady

Martha's been doing this since 1970 and when I arrived she was ironing. She is so calm, laid back, that any careworn day will be immediately put into context over a cup of tea and a gentle joke. She and John have a great sense of humour and work off each other (and some of their less mournful guests) delightfully. They are very interested in other people — Martha describes herself as an 'armchair traveller'. The farmhouse, built by Huguenots in 1772, is reached up a long drive. There is a big drawing room that manages to be cosy with all the furniture round the fire. Upstairs rooms have nice views, wooden beds, white shutters and plenty of space. If you're eating in then you dine together; with Martha's presence (when possible) and John's story-telling talents, these evenings are great fun. Not everyone can make this work. And dinner is one of Martha's specialities, focussing on vegetables and cheeses. This is real Irish country farmhouse accommodation.

Rooms: 5: 1 twin, 1 family and 1 single sharing 1 bathroom and shower; 1 twin with en suite shower; 1 twin with own bathroom.
Price: £23 — £25 p.p. Sing. supp. £5.
Breakfast: Included — full Irish.
Meals: Dinner £15. Packed lunches on request.
Closed: October 1st — March 1st (ring out of season).

How to get there: From Clones take Newbliss/Ballybay Rd (left of the Leonard Arms Hotel) (R183) for 6 km — house signed on the left before railway bridge.

Map Ref No: 8

Castle Leslie

Glaslough
Monaghan
Co. Monaghan

Tel: 047-88109
Fax: 047-88256
E-mail: ultan@castle-leslie.ie
www: www.castle-leslie.ie

Samantha Leslie and Ultan Bannon

Castle Leslie is like nowhere else — in the world. There may be other wonderful castles set in magnificent grounds with four lakes et al. But so often they are hotels. This house is a family home and everything there has been collected over 200 years; there is literally nothing to suggest you are in the 1990s. Many of the antiques were gathered during Sir John Leslie's 1850s grand tour, but practically everything catches the eye: the throne in the drawing room (in case the Pope came to visit); the view over the nearest lake; the copy of Michelangelo's cloister from Rome; the columned dining hall; the portraits of previous Leslies (and survivors) and related Churchills. And then the bedrooms that Sammy has created with exceptional flair and humour. There is a cathedral room, a haunted room, a bamboo room, Chinese, mauve... all are fascinating. The bathrooms too, with weird and wonderful Victorian loos and showers, the oldest tub in Ireland, a throne loo, an amazing hippy bathroom in psychedelic colours. Book yourself in; Sammy and Ultan couldn't be more down-to-earth and friendly. *Over 18s only — the Castle is X-rated!*

Rooms: 14: 13 doubles and 1 twin; 13 with en suite and 1 with bathroom/Victorian shower/sit-in bath.
Price: £52 — £68 p.p. Packages available for more than one night, with dinner etc. Single supp. £18.
Breakfast: Included — full Irish.
Meals: Dinner £25.50. Picnic lunches £10 — £17.50.

Closed: Open all year by arrangement with the banks

How to get there: From Monaghan follow signs to Armagh onto the N12. Left signed to R185, Glaslough. At Glaslough village, go through estate gates, past equestrian centre.

Map Ref No: 8

Fort Singleton

Emyvale
Co. Monaghan

Tel: 047-86054
Fax: 047-86120

Anne and Ray Goodall

Ray and Ann have completely and astonishingly restored this 1750s Georgian house themselves, working round anything original that was left. Ray is one of those people who see a piece of old junk in a skip and the next day it's a beautiful standard lamp that looks as though it's been in his drawing room since time began. The overgrown outbuildings at Fort Singleton are full of "stuff" waiting to be transformed. So the house today is fun and comfortable, with huge upstairs bedrooms looking onto surrounding hills and sheep fields. Downstairs rooms are 'wheelchair accessible' and definitely not recycled are the brand new mattresses. The furniture is quirky and antiquey — a half-tester, a brass bed, a carved frieze, a pianola, an old wireless. Outside there's a walled vegetable garden where Anne gathers her freshest ingredients for delicious candlelit dinners. Some of their many plans include the opening of a restaurant, a small lake and gardens accessible to wheelchair users. You know it will happen. They are such a nice couple with so much energy — and the results are always special.

Rooms: 6: 2 twins, 3 doubles and 1 triple: 1 with en suite bath, 5 with en suite shower.
Price: £25 p.p. Sing. supp. £5.
Breakfast: Included — full Irish.
Meals: Dinner £18.
Closed: December 23rd — 27th.

How to get there: From Monaghan take N2 for 6 miles towards Derry into Emyvale — through village, house signed 2nd left after 1 mile (10 minutes from Monaghan).

Map Ref No: 8

Dublin
•
Kildare
•
Wicklow
•

Dublin and South

Redbank Lodge and Restaurant

6 & 7 Church St, Skerries
Fingal
Co. Dublin

Tel: 01-849-1005
Fax: 01-849-1598
E-mail: redbank@tinet.ie
www: guesthouseireland.com

Terry and Margaret McCoy

Terry is dedicated to his own style, a Skerries fanatic, a mover and shaker in promoting this undervisited (in his view!) seaside region, President of the Irish Restaurants Association, an irrepressible original. He is also a very fine shellfish and seafood chef with an array of awards... if you want the opinion of others. But go and see for yourself. The restaurant is the mainstay of the place and ingredients are locally obtained where possible — freshest seafood from Skerries harbour, wonderful Dublin Bay prawns, even razorfish, normally seen as long empty shells on the beach. Apéritifs are in a warm ante-room where difficult decisions are taken with menus and an atmosphere of anticipation engendered. There are two buildings for B&Bers. The old bank house itself which adjoins the restaurant (the wine cellar is the old safe with its original door) is the most recently redecorated. Rooms have mod cons like TV and telephone, but also comfort with good quality beds. This is a great place for training into Dublin and avoiding the traffic... or for a last excellent meal before leaving Ireland from the nearby airport.

Rooms: 12: In bankhouse: 6 d and 1 tw, 3 en/s sh, 4 en/s bath. In lodge: 3 d and 2 tw, all en/s sh; 1 extra b'room.
Price: £25 — £35 p.p. Sing. supp. £10.
Breakfast: Included — full Irish.
Meals: Dinners in the restaurant start at 7: £26 and £28 set menus. Sunday lunch à la carte £15.75.
Closed: Christmas Eve, Christmas Day and Boxing Day.

How to get there: From Dublin take N1 to Blake's Cross, turn right signed to Skerries — follow for 10 km under bridge, first left, continue down. Church St on the right opposite Murray's Londis shop.

Map Ref No: 9

Belcamp Hutchinson

Malahide Rd
Balgriffin, Dublin 17
Co. Dublin

Tel: 01-846-0843
Fax: 01-848-5703

Doreen Gleeson

Dublin has been extending its girth right up to Belcamp Hutchinson's gravel front and lawns since 1786 when Francis Hely-Hutchinson originally built it, but it is probably still quicker to reach the city centre today (around 20 minutes to St Stephen's Green) than it was then. The house lies off the busy Malahide road (Malahide is a lovely village, by the way), but enclosed by high walls and surrounded by four acres of bird- and flower-filled garden so you can instantly forget this. The Gleesons are renovating the old walled garden, growing roses up trellises to form a tunnel; the hedge-maze may still be in its infancy when you visit. Three old dogs (I hope there are still three!) will good-naturedly usher you into Belcamp's Georgian interior. The feeling is of a small country house hotel and Doreen is tireless in her efforts to make sure guests are well looked after, collecting and dropping off from the nearby airport, letting me park my car there between trips! Wooden floors, big comfortable zip-and-link beds, strong plain colours, modern furnishings, immaculately tidy — fancy escaping from the city...?

Rooms: 8: 3 doubles/twins; 5 doubles; all with en suite bath.
Price: £44 p.p. No sing. supp.
Breakfast: Included — full Irish.
Meals: Available in Dublin.
Closed: December 23rd-30th.

How to get there: From Dublin take the Malahide Road out of the centre for about four miles. House signed off this road to the left. House second left. For more directions ask Doreen to fax you her details.

Map Ref No: 14

Ashbrook Country House

River Rd
Ashtown, Castleknock
Co. Dublin

Tel: 01-8385660
Fax: 01-8385660

Stan and Eve Mitchell

I visited Ashbrook on a beautiful sunny day and felt I was back in the country. You would never guess that you were in Dublin. This is a 200-year-old Georgian manor with lovely curved bay windows with their original glass and window seats. Doors give onto an immaculate lawn and grass tennis court, surrounded by trees. The canal passes by the end of the garden, although not visibly, and the property lies a good hammer throw from Phoenix Park. From the outside the house looks lovely, climbed by roses, with its curved section, white balustraded first-floor balcony and old, white, shuttered windows. The bedroom in the curved section is my favourite with its curved door and windows and narrow balcony. All the rooms are pretty, done in pale colours (pinks and creams) and all are very different. There are good views all round the house. Eve runs the B&B side of things and runs it with natural friendliness.

Rooms: 4: all double/twin with en suite showers. There is also an extra bathroom.
Price: £25 — £30 p.p. Sing. supp. £10.
Breakfast: Included — full Irish.
Meals: Recommends The Back Yard up the road.
Closed: Two weeks at Christmas and New Year.

How to get there: From the airport take M50 south. Exit at N3 turn-off for Blanchardstown. Left at roundabout and on to another roundabout. Straight on to Halfway House pub on left. Turn left at pub, over rail crossing, 1st left, house 2nd gate on left.

Map Ref No: 13

Kilronan House

70 Adelaide Rd
Dublin 2
Co. Dublin

Tel: 01-4755266
Fax: 01-4782841

Noel and Deirdre Comer

You wouldn't really want to be more central than this address, just round the corner from St Stephen's Green, but very peaceful and leafily residential. This is a well-to-do Georgian townhouse (1834), not grand but very comfortable with its original cornicing and ceiling roses. There was a slightly old-fashioned, almost self-consciously dated feel to Kilronan until Noel's overhaul last year which transformed the place. He opened up the two rooms on the ground floor which increased the space and light. He found lovely 1830s parquet flooring hidden under the old carpets. Big mirrors and wooden chairs now grace the new-look dining room, elegant armchairs adorn the sitting area, yellows and whites brighten inviting bedrooms...you wouldn't recognize the place. Meanwhile, Noel and Homer (the B&B labrador) continue to epitomise the gracious welcome. There aren't many places in Dublin where your hosts take such pains on your behalf, I can assure you. He is also a mine of information on where to go and what to do in Dublin and will direct guests with military precision. A very friendly retreat in a big city.

Rooms: 12: 2 singles; 2 family; 8 doubles.
All with with en suite facilities.
Price: £45 p.p. Sing. supp. £10.
Breakfast: Included — full Irish.
Meals: Available in Dublin. Recommends "Pier 32" and "Chapter 1".
Closed: Never!

How to get there: From St Stephen's Green go up Earlsford Terrace past the National Concert Hall, 50 metres, T-junction, turn right, 5th house on the right. Private secure parking.

Map Ref No: 14

Number 31

31 Leeson Close
Dublin 2
Co. Dublin

Tel: 01-6765011
Fax: 01-6762929

Noel Comer

You are right in the heart of the city by St Stephen's Green, a great place for eating out, pubs and sightseeing. Number 31 is run by an extremely friendly Noel whose presence makes the atmosphere here fun and upbeat. Noel knows that the personal touch in an anonymous city makes all the difference, and that has been the secret of his success at Kilronan, his other guesthouse. You enter this old coach house through a door in a mews into the reception, a sunken seating area with black leather banquettes, the walls studded with modern art. A great variety of rooms are spread over the two buildings: the coach house and its master, a fine Georgian townhouse looking onto Fitzwilliam Place. The Comers' famous guests can avoid reporters by entering via the mews, crossing the connecting garden and leaving from the other side (I found this very useful). The coach house rooms naturally have lower ceilings; some have their own little patio. The main house contains some huge rooms with original cornicing and plasterwork. Attention to detail and a genuine enjoyment of what he does make Noel a wonderful host. *Children over 10.*

Rooms: 18: all double or twin/triples; all with en suite bath except 3 with just shower.
Price: £35 — £55 p.p. Single from £45.
Breakfast: Included — full Irish.
Meals: Available in Dublin.
Closed: Christmas week.

How to get there: From St Stephen's Green go past the Shelbourne Hotel up Merrion Row, turn right at Pembroke St. At end turn left (Leeson St) — Leeson Close is first left. Nº31 has secure car parking.

Map Ref No: 14

Glenveagh Townhouse
31 Nothumberland Rd   **Tel:** 01-668-4612
Ballsbridge
Co. Dublin

Winnie Cunningham

A late 1890s Victorian house set back from the road with its own parking and, as with so many of the best places to stay in the capital, it's in Ballsbridge — an elegant address. The dining and sitting rooms have high ceilings, intricate cornicing and ceiling roses, dark-pink comfy sofas, gilt mirrors. Bedrooms here typically have the high ceilings too, with thick carpets, white duvets, TVs and phones etc, and huge pelmeted and curtained windows. But there is wide variety. Some are smaller and sweeter, the lower ground floor level is more brightly decorated to compensate for lower ground floor light, and there is a modern extension at the back — but all have the personal stamp, all are large and there are none that aren't attractive. They are kept immaculate by Winnie who has recently taken over the running of this long-standing family concern. It is a professional place but friendly with it. Breakfasts — which can be taken in bed — are fresh, and full cooked breakfast is to order, a luxury you wouldn't often find in London these days. This is a well-established, elegant townhouse near where you want to be.

Rooms: 13: 3 family, 6 doubles, 4 twins, all with en suite bath or shower.
Price: £30 — £40 p.p. (£50 during rugby internationals!). Sing. supp. £10.
Breakfast: Included — full Irish.
Meals: Several good restaurants in the area.
Closed: One week at Christmas.

How to get there: From Trinity College follow Nassau St which becomes Mount St, then Northumberland Rd — parking by the house.

Map Ref No: 14

Waterloo House

8 — 10 Waterloo Rd
Ballsbridge, Dublin 4
Co. Dublin

Tel: 01-660-1888
Fax: 01-667-1955
E-mail: waterloohouse@tinet.ie

Evelyn Corcoran

Waterloo is two large 1830s Georgian houses with twin doors like close-knit eyes to welcome you in. This is their first year in operation and Evelyn and crew are very keen to make sure guests are not treated as bednights. Evelyn's background is in hotels and elements of Waterloo are hotelly — there are 17 rooms after all, and the odd trouser press lurks furtively in the shadows. But the welcome is sincere and friendly and that is such a relief in a popular big city like Dublin. Everything here is clean and tidy, immaculately so. Bedrooms have thick carpets, reproduction furniture, good-sized bathrooms (although baths themselves are not enormous) with little shampoos etc. Everything is brand new so should be in perfect working order. Common rooms include a comfortable sitting area-cum-reception, a dining room with plush patterned carpets where extensive Irish breakfasts take place, a wicker-seated conservatory. It's a lovely, high-ceilinged house in a peaceful-yet-central part of the city — and it is managed with friendly professionalism. *Parking for 8 cars in front of house.*

Rooms: 17: 5 twins and 12 doubles; 9 with en suite bath, 8 with en suite shower.
Price: £37.50 — £45 p.p. Sing. supp. £8.50 — £15.
Breakfast: Included — full Irish.
Meals: Great restaurants abound in the area.
Closed: December 23rd — 28th.

How to get there: From St Stephen's Green take Merrion Row which becomes Baggott St, then Upper Baggott St. First right after bridge is Waterloo Rd. House is on left.

Map Ref No: 14

Simmonstown House

2 Sydenham Rd
Ballsbridge, Dublin 4
Co. Dublin

Tel: 01-6607260
Fax: 01-6607341

Finola and James Curry

James — who has returned permanently and with relief from years of overseas
business — and Finola are great hosts. And this is a lovely private home in Dublin 4.
It was a pleasure for me anyway, after a stressful day, to find myself sitting in the
soothing elegance of the drawing room with its marble fireplace, gilt mirror, plush
curtains, deep blues and purples, chatting away over gin and tonics. *Were* they old
friends? I don't think there are many places as civilised in Dublin. We were treated
later to some live gospel singing in the drawing room, courtesy of other guests with
more talent. I cannot guarantee this will happen when you stay, but it was typical of
the friendly atmosphere at Simmonstown. The rooms have been done to a high
degree of comfort with light-yet-warm duvets and bright shining bathrooms. The
other major draw at Simmonstown — something you should leave time and space
for — are the sumptuous breakfasts. Everything was so beautifully arranged it
seemed a shame to disturb it. Somehow we found the nerve. *Simmonstown has cots
for kids.*

Rooms: 4: 2 twins, 1 single/double and 1
double/family, all with en suite shower.
Price: £40 — £50 p.p. Sing supp £10.
Breakfast: Included — full Irish.
Meals: Good local restaurants.
Closed: December 20th — January 4th.

How to get there: Ask when booking as
it's in central Dublin.

Map Ref No: 14

Moytura House

Saval Park Rd
Dalkey
Co. Dublin

Tel: 01-285-2371
Fax: 01-235-0633
E-mail: giacomet@indigo.ie
www: http:/www.indigo.ie.hiddenireland/29.html

Alain and Corinne Giacometti

He's a French architect with an Italian name and she's an Irish interior architect with a French name. These days Corinne has her day filled for her by a friendly young family and equally friendly guests... I hope. She does this with such grace and humour that you will feel immediately involved in the life of the household, however short your stay. Alain is equally charming and may, if you are lucky, rise from his elevations to show you the high roads of Dalkey on the back of his two-seater Harley. He obviously can't be expected to do this for everyone! The house (1881 — John Loftus Robinson) is wonderful, hidden in trees and perched on a hill. Guest rooms are large and square with big beds, modern pictures, thick carpets, ivy-framed windows, and one looks out to sea — very inviting. Downstairs there are elegant tapestries on walls, rugs on floors, sofas to sit on, a round wooden table for breakfast — the place was designed to be lived in, not merely looked at. This is a lovely area and yet only 30 minutes from St Stephen's Green. And what a nice family to welcome you to Ireland.

Rooms: 3: 2 doubles and 1 double/twin, 2 with en suite bath, 1 with en suite shower.
Price: £40 p.p. Sing. supp. £15.
Breakfast: Included — full Irish.
Meals: Many excellent restaurants in Dalkey.
Closed: September 30th — April 1st.

How to get there: From Dunlaoghaire go into Dalkey. Right at T-junction and up Barnhill Rd. Saval Park Rd is 4th on left, house immediately on right among trees.

Map Ref No: 14

Druid Lodge

Killiney Hill Rd
Killiney
Co. Dublin

Tel: 01-285-1632
Fax: 01-284-8504

Ken and Cynthia McClenaghan

The Dalkey/Killiney area of County Dublin has been compared to the French Riviera with its corniche roads winding round blue bays... and all those nice houses. And Druid Lodge (1832) is one of the best of them. On a beautiful day there's not much that doesn't catch the eye, inside or out. The house and tangled garden look straight out to sea and the views from upstairs bedrooms and the first-floor, creeper-strangled balcony are transfixing. There is an eclectic eye at work: the unusual, the arcane and the merely beautiful grab the visitor's attention from all sides at once — amazing overmantles in ebony with bevelled glass mirrors, Africana from Ken's long years as a sociologist on that continent, figurines, leather masks and more modern paintings for contrast. But this is not some museum to ponder in silence. Ken and Cynthia are full of chat and they have gone to great lengths to make bedrooms really special, particularly the largest first-floor rooms with the views. These are spectacular, although none would disappoint. A really entertaining house.

Rooms: 4: 2 doubles and 2 doubles/twins, all with en suite shower.
Price: £28 — £35 p.p. Sing. supp. £7.
Breakfast: Included — full Irish.
Meals: Good restaurants in Dalkey.
Closed: December 24th — 28th.

How to get there: Follow signs for Dunlaoghaire ferry. From ferry follow signs for Killiney via Dalkey. Entrance to lodge between Druid's Chair pub and Killiney Avenue oppostite white stones.

Map Ref No: 14

Martinstown House

The Curragh, Kildare
Co. Kildare

Tel: 045-441269
Fax: 045-441208

Meryl Long

Martinstown is something very different for Ireland. There is Meryl who has great energy and character and who settles easily and deeply into conversation with her guests; the house itself, which is fascinating; and the charming, well-maintained garden and grounds. Originally part of the huge estates of the Dukes of Leinster, the house was completed by the Burrowes family between 1832 and 1840 in the Gothic style as a *cottage orné*. The whole place is a flight of fancy with many surprises — like the drawing/ballroom which has a ceiling that is twice as high as the rest of the ground floor. The house today bubbles with vitality, is beautifully decorated and the overall style is informal and elegant — old-fashioned hospitality mixed with a high degree of modern comfort. Guests all eat together and whenever possible Meryl joins them. Dinners are often centred on big roasts. This is a family home and I consider it great value. *Racing nearby. Unsuitable for young children.*

Rooms: 4: 1 twin en suite bathroom; 1 twin own bathroom; 1 double en suite bathroom; 1 double own shower.
Price: £45 — £60 p.p. Sing. supp. £10.
Breakfast: Included — full Irish.
Meals: Dinner £28 (8 p.m. Please book by midday).
Closed: December 16th — January 7th.

How to get there: From Dublin N7/M7 south. Follow to N9, exit at Kilcullen, turn R on N78 to Athy. 1 mile turn R signed Martinstown. 1.5 miles turn L opposite Ballysax Church. 0.5 mile to stone entrance and cattle grid on L.

Map Ref No: 13

Tonlegee House and Restaurant

Athy
Co. Kildare

Tel: 0507-31473
Fax: 0507-31473

Mark and Marjorie Molloy

The food at Tonlegee is prepared with tender loving care by Mark Molloy; listen to the rave reports of those who've already been... and who will no doubt be back. The carefully chosen menu caters for all tastes, although Mark prefers those who order his more exotic creations. And with such a fine chef in the kitchen it is a great opportunity to try something new. Here's a couple from the menu on the day I visited: 'roast fillet of hake with tapenade and red pepper sauce' as a starter; 'breast of guinea fowl and a ballotine of its leg, with bacon and spring cabbage' for the main course. Everything is prepared on the premises. The house, sitting on five acres of garden, was built in 1790, and has Georgian architraves, a lovely curved-ceiling landing and a Victorian extension. Bedrooms are large and antiquely furnished with all mod cons, so there is great comfort — deep blue carpets and yellow walls. Room nine is particularly tempting, huge and with a sitting area and equally huge bathroom with free-standing bath. Go for a walk along the canal, come back for a deep luxurious soak, have a pre-prandial drink in the drawing room by the fire... and then dinner.

Rooms: 9: 6 doubles and 3 doubles/ twins, all with en suite baths, except 1 with shower only.
Price: £37.50 p.p. Sing. supp. £15.
Breakfast: Included — full Irish.
Meals: Dinner about £23 (set menu and à la carte).
Closed: First two weeks of November, Christmas and New Year.

How to get there: From Dublin take M7 towards Naas — 2nd exit after Naas onto M9 towards Waterford. Next exit onto N78 to Athy — over the three bridges, first left after Tegral, signed to Tonlegee. 0.5 miles to house.

Map Ref No: 13

Griesemount

Ballitore
Co. Kildare

Tel: 0507-23158
Fax: 0503-40687
E-mail: griesemount@tinet.ie

Robert and Carolyn Ashe

This well-proportioned old house (1817) sits on top of a hill near a Quaker village with lovely views (even from the bathrooms) over the walled garden and downhill to the River Griese and a ruined water mill. It is surrounded by charming outbuildings, with paddocks running down to the river. This is horse country and Carolyn was organising children at the stables when I arrived. The lovely sunny breakfast room matches Carolyn's personality — she's warm, chatty and enjoys people so much she could say in all honesty that she'd never had anyone staying she hadn't liked! The house is full of creaky stairs and floorboards and quaint touches such as the soldier sculpture in the hall and the bookshelves tucked under window sills in bedrooms. These are all interesting, with nice views, a great half-tester, a library bathroom with matting floor and a screen round the bath. The drawing room is well lived-in; low, oft-sat-upon furniture crowds round the fireplace — the grand piano is there to be played. The Ashes hope you will adopt the house as you find it — according to proper bed and breakfast tradition.

Rooms: 2: 1 double with en suite bath and 1 with own bath.
Price: £20 — £30 p.p. (third night free!).
Breakfast: Included — full Irish.
Meals: Good choice available locally.
Closed: December 1st — February 15th.

How to get there: From Dublin take N7 off N50 towards Naas for 20 miles, then M9 towards Carlow/Kilkenny. Go 12 miles; 1 mile after Texaco garage small road to right signed Griesemount. First house on left.

Map Ref No: 13

Kilkea Lodge Farm

Kilkea
Castledermot
Co. Kildare

Tel: 0503-45112
Fax: 0503-45112

Godfrey and Marion Greene

Up a longish drive, surrounded by paddocks and stables, with long views over undulating fields of corn, sits Kilkea Lodge Farm, substantial, yet cosy. Marion and Godfrey are the present incumbents of a house built by previous Greenes in 1740. They clearly love having people around. 'Take us as you find us' is the motto here, and it is important to them that you do; Kilkea is definitely a family home. Enter this farmhouse through a conservatory-porch and pass the boaters and panamas in the hall stand. The drawing room is wonderfully informal: old leather-bound books along the walls, framed family photos, a tiled fire, bay window, hairy rugs on the backs of sit-in-me sofas and armchairs. And along the upstairs corridors are the very various rooms. Mine was womb-like, a boudoir, with big comfortable bed and many layers of bedclothes, pillows everwhere; then there's the wonderful house-sized family room with rocking horse, two double beds, two singles, a piano, a cot, flower-baskets, a patchwork quilt on the wall, screens, wicker. It's "fun", says Marion. Indeed, a lovely house with history and atmosphere.

Rooms: 4: 1 double with en/s shower; 1 double with own bathroom;1 twin with own shower; 1 family/studio with hip-bath and shower.
Price: From £30 p.p. Sing. supp. £5 in high season.
Breakfast: Included — full Irish.
Meals: Dinner £20. Supper £15.
Closed: December. Open at New Year by arrangement.

How to get there: From Carlow take N9 direction Dublin to Castledermot (7 miles). In centre of town turn left signed Kilkea. Stay right of the butcher's, follow road for 2 miles, over hump-backed bridge. House opposite on left up long avenue.

Map Ref No: 13

Rathsallagh House

Dunlavin
Co. Wicklow

Tel: 045-403112
Fax: 045-403343

Joe and Kay O'Flynn

This is a country house hotel, rarely a genre that appeals to me. But what a gem is Rathsallagh! Somehow, despite the hotel's bustle, the 18-hole championship golf course and the heated indoor swimming pool and sauna, *somehow* this manages to feel like a home from home. Staff are friendly, fires crackle in hearths between carved elephants... the place even smells homely. Food at Rathsallagh is done to a T. Many of the ingredients are plucked from the beautiful mature walled garden — there's a full-grown sequoia in there with the fruit and veg. They keep their own free-range pigs for home-made rashers, the courtyard walls are full of herbs... you get the idea. They want to do it themselves. And every room is a delight. Often wide and short with many windows, they have either the long-distance view over parkland, or the equally lovely garden shot for the more myopic. No two rooms are the same. Some have their own access to the garden, one its own sitting room, one a Tardis-shower which even does foot massage. And all the O'Flynns have their own field of expertise which they exercise with easy-going friendliness.

Rooms: 17: 6 twins and 11 doubles; all with en suite bath, some with bath and shower.
Price: £55 — £95 p.p. Sing supp. £30 — £50.
Breakfast: Included — full Irish.
Meals: Dinner £30 — £35.
Closed: December 23rd — 27th, January 7th — 31st.

How to get there: From S. Dublin go to Tallacht and take Blessington Rd south. Straight through Blessington on Baltinglass Rd and follow for 6 miles. Right at Toughers petrol station for Dunlavin. In Dunlavin turn right and follow rd for 2.5 miles. Rathsallagh is on left.

Map Ref No: 13

99

The Manor

Manor Kilbride
Blessington
Co. Wicklow

Tel: 01-4582105
Fax: 01-4582607

Charles and Margaret Cully

The Manor, a wonderful Heritage House built in the 1820s, is hidden among 42 of its own acres. The drive there is one of the most lovely in Ireland, through thick wood, rhododendron, bamboo, over the river, ferns and leaves brushing your windscreen. Practically everything you encounter at The Manor is either of aesthetic, natural or artistic interest and behind it all are Charles and Margaret, great entertainers and easy-going. There are long walks around the two lakes, well stocked with trout; there's a swimming pool-cum-greenhouse, views over the Wicklow Mountains and three sweet little self-catering cottages with their own gardens. The interior has some outstanding features, too: the drawing room with its sixteen panels by the famous maritime artist Edwin Hayes; or the dark-red 1820 dining room now resurrected after an art-restorer daughter removed five layers of wallpaper until she found the original Morroccan leather. The film 'Widow's Peak', starring Mia Farrow, was shot here. Bedrooms are old-fashioned, uncluttered, with great beds, fabulous views, all with real bathrooms. *French and Spanish spoken.*

Rooms: 5: 1 double with en suite bath; 2 twins with en suite bath; 2 twins with own bath. One cottage is 'wheelchair friendly'.
Price: £50 — £60 p.p. No sing. supp.
Breakfast: Included — full Irish.
Meals: Dinner from £21.
Closed: October 1st — April 1st. (Cottages available all year — out of season groups book in advance.)

How to get there: On N81, 7 km north of Blessington take Kilbride/Sallygap turn. After 2 km turn left at Sallygap sign. Entrance gates 50m on right.

Map Ref No: 13

Mitchell's Restaurant and Guesthouse

Laragh
Glendalough
Co. Wicklow

Tel: 0404-45302
Fax: 0404-45302

Jerry and Margaret Mitchell

The Mitchells are an old Wicklow family with a certain fame in the world of catering; Jerry's grandfather ran the celebrated Mitchells in Dublin. The old magic's still there, in this charming eatery right in the heart of the mountains, minutes from Glendalough. Downstairs, wooden tables stand on a tiled floor and there was a happy buzz from a full house when I visited. It is hard to imagine the tumbledown shack that Jerry and Margaret originally bought. Single-minded dedication won them the lovely wrought-iron trellised windows, no two of which are exactly the same. There is a sitting room, too, for after-dinner or -lunch coffees on white-upholstered chairs. Margaret's food is wonderful and they've won awards for their wholemeal and sunflower seed bread. Both she and Jerry have ploughed huge amounts of themselves into this restaurant with rooms. These last are in pine, small, two have skylight windows (so, unfortunately, the wonderful view is not made full use of), plain wood furniture and comfortable beds. Outside there's a little terrace whereupon to sit with coffee and gaze at the Wicklow Mountains. *No children under 12.*

Rooms: 4: 2 doubles and 2 twins, all with en suite shower.
Price: £20 p.p. Sing. supp. £6 — £18.50.
Breakfast: Included — full Irish.
Meals: Lunch (not Sundays) à la carte, main course about £7. Sunday lunch £13.50. Dinner £20.
Closed: Three weeks in January and Christmas.

How to get there: From Dublin take N11 to Kilmacanogue. Turn right for Glendalough. In Laragh bear right and house is on right.

Map Ref No: 13

Derrybawn House

Glendalough
Co. Wicklow

Tel: 0404-45134
Fax: 0404-45109

Donald and Lucy Vambeck

Approach Derrybawn House along the rollercoaster mountain roads set deep in trees that dapple the of light. Built in 1780 in the forested heart of the Wicklow Mountains as part of a sporting estate, the house has a panoramic backdrop of wooded hills and is surrounded by paddocks, lawns, a lake and mature trees. There's a heavenly sense of peace. Enter through the trellised porch covered in vines; on a hot day floor-to-ceiling windows become doors to step through too. The dining room — where guests eat round a large table that seats twelve — has floor-boards, a big rug and tall, inward-opening casement windows. Take pre-dinner drinks in the pretty, wicker-furnished morning room. The house is far larger than you would imagine from the front and the full tour seemed to go on and on, to the big billiards room upstairs at the end of a very long corridor. Bedrooms are all interesting, with barrel ceilings, pretty windows and mirrors, power showers; one has a jacuzzi bath, although the style is resolutely country cottage. There are also two grander rooms with high ceilings, armchairs, a four-poster and that view beyond the walled flower gardens....

Rooms: 6: 2 doubles with en suite bath; 2 doubles with en suite shower; 2 twins with en suite shower.
Price: £27.50 — £32.50 p.p. Sing. supp. £12.50.
Breakfast: Included — full Irish.
Meals: Dinner (for groups by arrangement) £17.50.
Closed: December 22nd — 28th.

How to get there: From Dublin take N11 to Kilmacanoge (R755). Follow signs to Glendalough. In Laragh turn left (R755). House on right after 0.5 miles.

Map Ref No: 13

Plattenstown House

Coolgreaney Rd
Arklow
Co. Wicklow

Tel: 0402-37822
Fax: 0402-37822

Margaret McDowell

Margaret is absolutely dedicated to the care of her guests and is very gracious with it, taking (quite naturally) great pride in the hordes of returning people that she sees as friends rather than customers. She has counted 26 nationalities passing through so far and enjoys seeing people from different backgrounds getting together, whether it be over dinner or her very complete breakfast. This is not a TV-in-the-bedroom sort of place. She is also very up on what to do in this fascinating region: there's historic Arklow with its Parnell connection; the area is a golfer's paradise; there are lovely beaches with golden sand and little coves for swimming; and then the forestry and hill-walking. The house itself has a shallow bay window (upstairs and down) from which you look over lovely mature gardens with palms and rhododendrons and wrought-iron seats. Bedrooms are just fine, with zip-and-link beds and thick carpets. *Ask about children.*

Rooms: 4: 2 doubles/twins with en suite showers; 1 twin with private bathroom; 1 double with en suite shower.
Price: £21 — £25 p.p. Sing. supp. £6.
Breakfast: Included — full Irish.
Meals: Dinner £16.
Closed: November 1st — March 1st except by arrangement.

How to get there: From Dublin take N11 for 45 miles to Arklow, straight up through town to small roundabout, across to Coolgreany Road. House 3 miles on left.

Map Ref No: 14

Laois
•
Offaly
•
Tipperary
•

The South Midlands

Preston House

Main St
Abbeyleix
Co. Laois

Tel: 0502-31432/31662
Fax: 0502-31432

Alison and Michael Dowling

Preston House is an ivy-clad Georgian pile on the main road of this 'heritage' town. It's the old schoolhouse, and the residents' dining room was the head's study. No doubt generations of children have knocked and entered with some trepidation, but it couldn't be more welcoming nowadays. Alison is warm, smiley and instantly draws you into the jolly atmosphere of this place. The house is a family home, but also has a busy café with wooden tables, a piano, attractive lighting, creaky pine floorboards, a big old school cupboard and a fire in winter. Upstairs there is another wonderful huge classroom, now a bare space with a raised bannistered section where choirs and musicians used to perform. There are plans for art exhibitions or musical evenings there. The bedrooms are large with big comfy wooden beds, sofas, magazines and pine plank floors scattered with rugs. The old-style sitting room is a quiet space in this bustling house.

Rooms: 4: all doubles/twins with en suite showers.
Price: £25 p.p.
Breakfast: Included — full Irish.
Meals: Lunches about £7 — £9 à la carte. Dinner £15 — £16 à la carte.
Closed: For the 10 days after Christmas.

How to get there: From Dublin take N7 south towards Portlaoise — for 65 miles. Then N8 south to Abbeyleix — house on the main road.

Map Ref No: 12

Tullanisk
Birr
Co. Offaly

Tel: 0509-20572
Fax: 0509-21783
E-mail: tnisk@indigo.ie

Susie and George Gossip

Don't be scared if George, aproned and brusque in red beard and green cords, is the first to appear from his infernal kitchen. His bark is worse than his bite. In fact my first bite was a mouth-melting poached pear, Cashel blue cheese and watercress affair followed by a very tender beef stroganoff. Opinions are aired freely at table so don't hold back — your chances are fair on most subjects but tackle shooting or architectural history at your peril. The house has been carefully restored — beautifully painted plaster mouldings — and flagstoned halls and stairs brightened with a happy yellow. They are proud, too, of some unusual fireplaces, especially a kind of gold and blue porthole that beams benignly in the drawing room. The rooms are snug and open to big window views of the gorgeous park, part of Birr Castle Estate. My abiding memory is of the deer at dawn breaking from the woods like a wave across the misty green pasture. George offers cheaper deals for longer stays.

Rooms: 7: 2 twins and 3 doubles, all with en suite bath; 1 twin and 1 double sharing shower room.
Price: £38 — £50 p.p. (lower prices for 2 nights or more). Sing. supp. £10.
Breakfast: Included — full Irish.
Meals: Dinner £25. Packed lunches on request.
Closed: Mid-December — 29th.

How to get there: From Birr take R439 direction Banagher. Gates on right after 1 mile.

Map Ref No: 12

Spinner's Town House
Birr
Co. Offaly

Tel: 0509-21673
Fax: 0509-21673
E-mail: spinners@indigo.ie
www: http://www.spinners-townhouse.com

Fiona and Joe Breen

Uniquely more than just a guest house — Fiona (ex fashion clothing) and Joe (builder) Breen have turned these five central Georgian town houses under the walls of Birr Castle into a chic bohemian centre. A popular theatre space, a bistro, a collection of abstract Irish art, an old stone courtyard (coffee hang-out) and the hostelry. This latter is all pine floors, orthopaedic beds and white Egyptian cotton linen. Everything is kept simple and new-looking. Castle Birr next door is famous for its gardens and leviathan telescope (which was the reason for Patrick Moore's visit: "I greatly enjoyed my stay"). The whole place is wonderful value — I doubt you'd find anything as interesting or genuinely fun as Spinners at their prices anywhere in Ireland. The upbeat bistro serves delicious food, breakfast is made by Joe of free-range and fresh ingredients (eggs, bacon, fresh orange, mackerel, croissants) and all the Spinners staff seem happy to be there. Let them point you down the road to Craughwell's pub after dinner. It's a local place and full of atmosphere, in keeping with the whole philosophy at Spinners.

Rooms: 9: 6 double/twins and 1 twin with en suite shower; 1 twin and 1 double with private shower.
Price: £17.50 — £20 p.p. Sing. supp. £5 dependent on season.
Breakfast: Included — full Irish.
Meals: Restaurant dinners à la carte: average price for 3 courses £16.
Closed: Nov 1st — March 16th. But groups all year.

How to get there: In Birr. From Emmet Square go down Main St past Benny Larkins shop. At the end of the street turn right in second square — house at end of road on the right.

Map Ref No: 12

Pine Lodge

Ross Rd
Screggan, Tullamore
Co. Offaly

Tel: 0506-51927
Fax: 0506-51927
E-mail: pinelodgehealth@tinet.ie

Claudia Krygel

"Suggested items to pack: Tracksuit, Weather Gear, Sturdy Shoes (for walking), Flip flops, Swimming costume, Hat & Towel" — so says Claudia's brochure for her fitness breaks. This doesn't mean you have to undergo two days of army-style regimen; quite the opposite. This is a chance to float downstream and be pampered. There are a sauna and steam bath, an indoor swimming pool, a sunbed. Massage, yoga and reflexology are available and special diets well organised. Claudia's breakfasts have won prizes to boot. It's a well-ordered house with wood everywhere, particularly stripped pine which Claudia adores — the house name is a happy coincidence. The main living space of the house is the open-plan kitchen, breakfast area and cordoned-off nest for watching TV or reading on sofas in front of the fire. The bedrooms all lie off one corridor and have low wooden beds, duvets, pine ceilings, excellent showers, wooden windows, good-sized towels. Claudia herself is intelligent, direct, fun and assiduous in keeping her ship tight. Her guests are the ones to benefit. *Minimum stay 2 nights.*

Rooms: 4: 1 double with en suite bath; 1 double with en suite shower; 2 twins with en suite shower.
Price: £25 p.p. Sing. supp. £5.
Breakfast: Included — full Irish.
Meals: Dinner with 24 hours notice: £23.
Closed: December 15th — February 15th.

How to get there: In Tullamore take N52 direction Birr. Keep right on main road when road forks 1 mile out of town. 2 miles further signed left to house. Pine Lodge is 0.5 miles on left.

Map Ref No: 12

Riverrun House

Terryglass
Co. Tipperary

Tel: 067-22125
Fax: 067-22187
E-mail: riverrun@iol.ie

Lucy and Tom Sanders

Tom and Lucy really have put down roots in the tiny, lake-favoured village of Terryglass. They started by remodelling a derelict church as a studio (he's a potter), shop and home. Then they built Riverrun just by the old stone bridge with salvaged slates and real sensitivity. The rooms are brightly, simply painted and full of air and light. Downstairs, they have split doors so you can lean out into their lovingly-tended, herbaceously colourful garden while keeping your feet on the seagrass matting. Apparently, in the summer this quiet village is busy with the Dublin weekend watersports crowd; I for one would certainly travel a lot further than the 50 yards I did just for the rather special food (try the home-marinated salmon; try anything) at "The Derg Inn" next door to Paddy's Bar. At either you may well find yourself settling for a long session so don't be alarmed if it's gone past time and the Gardaí show up. If the village is just too frantic you can always play a game of tennis, go for a bike ride or escape onto the lake in one of the owners' two motorised lakeboats. *Three charming self-catering cottages also now available.*

Rooms: 6: 2 twins; 2 doubles; 2 family: all en suite with bath and power shower.
Price: £25 p.p. Sing. supp. £7.50.
Breakfast: Included — full Irish.
Meals: Not available.
Closed: December 24th and 25th.

How to get there: From Nenagh take N52 to Borrisokane (12 miles). Left in village signed Ballinderry (5 miles). Right in village signed Terryglass (2 miles). House in centre of village on bridge.

Map Ref No: 11

108

Ashley Park House

Nenagh
Co. Tipperary

Tel: 067-38223
Fax: 067-38223
E-mail: david.mackenzie@compuserve.com

PJ and Margaret (daughter) Mounsey

There is a tangible feel of the past at Ashley Park, so far removed from any hustle and bustle, and it is a near-museum of brilliantly preserved antiquity. The bathrooms are elegantly Victorian with chessboard chequered floors and all the original metal and enamel. Bedrooms are big, the beds deeply carved. Downstairs, the air tastes smoky from many winters' peat fires and quiet rooms are full of rich, gleaming, dark floors and furniture. Dark, too, are the bold vines that curl up antique wallpapers. The conservatory (the "relaxing room") is lighter, and out on the Indian colonial verandah tea is served while you ponder the ruins of the island castle on their lake. When Sean is asked about the fairy fort in the woods he replies coyly, "There may be something in it". Outside, there are amazing, intact, ancient outbuildings. They rent the stone-built stables to a horse trainer and the cobbled, high-walled farmyard is home to peacocks, guineafowl, duck, hens and a dovecote. The surrounding woods are a nature reserve — look out for red squirrel in 300-year-old trees — and you can fish on the lake.

Rooms: 6: 1 family, 2 twins and 3 doubles: 4 sharing a bathroom, 2 en suite.
Price: £20 p.p. Sing. supp. £5.
Breakfast: Included — full Irish.
Meals: Dinner £18 on request.
Closed: Never!

How to get there: 3.5 miles from Nenagh towards Borrisokane, on left. Big house on lake signed from road.

109

Map Ref No: 11

Ballycormac House

Aglish
Borrisokane
Co. Tipperary

Tel: 067-21129
Fax: 067-21200

John and Cherylynn Lang

"After six years of visiting Ireland with increasing frequency, and inevitably going home with yet another horse, we decided it would be cheaper to live here." Good news for guests of the (English) Langs, some of whom may have visited this most unusual home when it was run by the (American) Quigleys. The building itself (a converted and extended dairy) is a warren of tiny passages, low doorways and sweet staircases. The house makes everybody feel tall and won't mind if I call it quaint. Bathrooms are sort of in there with you, screened off with saloon doors, and the beds are solid structures designed to be slept in. You will be warm and comfortable. And well fed. Cherylynn makes full use of their home-grown organic fruit and veg her culinary wonders to perform. They are an effusive couple and well suited to the Irish cráic. Finally, their obsession with horses is infectious and even I was cajoled onto a horse. They are highly professional (and persuasive — if you aren't confident take heart from me!) and the five-day treks, B&Bing back at base, are a wonderful way to see the local countryside.

Rooms: 5: 2 doubles with en suite bath; 2 twins with en suite bath; 1 single with private bath.
Price: £25 p.p. No sing supp.
Breakfast: Included — full Irish.
Meals: Dinner £20. Packed lunches for riders by arrangement.
Closed: Never!

How to get there: From Nenagh take N52 towards Portuma. 12 miles to Borrisokane. 0.25 miles on Ballycormac Rd signs to right. Turn and follow signs through Aglish to house.

Map Ref No: 12

Inch House

Thurles
Co. Tipperary

Tel: 0504-51348/51261
Fax: 0504-51754
E-mail: inchhse@iol.ie
www: http://iol.ie/tipp/inch-house.htm

The Egan Family

Inch House emerges stately from behind its stand of beeches, a promise of comfort in an arable plain — and how sumptuous it is. Nora, a former nurse, is the neat, practical one while John, the farmer, bursts with grand plans. The Egans have for twelve years tirelessly renovated to create a spacious temple of ease and good taste — country living in the grand style. From the fine relief of the serpent ceiling-roses to the 44-foot pitch pine floorboards in the William Morris-papered blue, white and gilt drawing room, all is complete. Ascend the wide, bifurcated, oak staircase past the rich stained glass of the Ryan family motto, "Death rather than Dishonour". The Ryans mysteriously stayed on as their fellow Catholics were dispossessed by Cromwell's penal law. You may relax happily, reclining on the finest linen in a Prince Albert bed or soaking in a wood-panelled bathroom; or you may linger over an exquisite breakfast or dinner, served on silver in the impressive restaurant. Most recently restored is the chapel where one of John's priest brothers may be saying mass....

Rooms: 5: 2 doubles and 3 twins: all with en suite bath.
Price: £28 p.p. Sing. supp. £5.
Breakfast: Included — full Irish.
Meals: Restaurant dinner £23.50.
Closed: Christmas.

How to get there: From N8 (Dublin — Cork road) take turn-off into Thurles, through square, onto Nenagh road. The drive is on the left after 4 miles, just past "The Ragg" crossroads.

111

Ardmayle House

Cashel
Co. Tipperary

Tel: 0504-42399
Fax: 0504-42420
E-mail: ardmayle@iol.ie
www: http://www.iol.ie/tipp/ardmayl.htm

Annette Hunt

This very pretty and rather unusual L-shaped Georgian farmhouse is home to Annette's young and active family. There's lots for the children to do at Ardmayle: swings, slides, a football goal and the farmyard, paddock and stables (which include a milking parlour) to investigate — *but they must be accompanied by an adult.* Further off down their own fenced path are one and a half miles of River Suir bank where an adult interest might stretch to some excellent fly fishing. Annette can help with advice on what flies to use. In the house all is carefully arranged between the heavy walls, a lighter touch given by the pink carpet. She has added a pine library and conservatory dining room — the bright-painted, wooden flowers are hers too, as are the bubbling enthusiasm and the unselfconscious welcome. Happy feelings are shared by guests who leave gifts of watercolours and drawings, hung on the yellow-painted upstairs passageway. The aesthete in you, too, will find the dramatic, distant silhouette of St Patrick's rock forever memorable.

Rooms: 5: 1 family (i.e. 1 double & 2 single beds) and 3 double en suites;1 double with own private bathroom.
Price: £19.50 p.p. Sing. supp. £6.50.
Breakfast: Included — full Irish.
Meals: Dinner £14.50 by arrangement only, but there are great restaurants in Cashel.
Closed: October 1st — April 1st.

How to get there: In Cashel centre thro' town towards Dublin. Just before N8 leaves town keep L at Rock House souvenir shop and straight on down hill (the middle of three roads). At bottom of hill L to Ardmayle (signed). Thro' village to house.

Map Ref No: 12

Bansha House

Bansha
Tipperary
Co. Tipperary

Tel: 062-54194
Fax: 062-54215

John and Mary Marnane

Like me you'll probably dawdle in the kitchen of this handsome early Georgian farmhouse. Mary likes to invite her guests in to find out what they need and chat occurs naturally in the house over wholesome breakfasts eaten together. Horses are sacred at Bansha and the equestrian centre is so busy there are bound to be others about the place too. Inside, the house has heavy thick walls and an informal drawing room warmed by a log fire. On the stairs you pass a row of Norman Rockwell prints on your way to the square pastel bedrooms with their cupboard showers — clean and comfortable. The couple of rooms that do not have bathrooms en suite are perhaps the nicest (often the case). Everything here sits prettily among old creeper-clad walls in the middle of paddocks with horses training or lazily munching. A fine scene for the artist. The house comes first, however, at Bansha, horses second — and it's a rare luxury to find somewhere the kids will love too. There is also great walking in the Galtees and the Glen of Aherlow. Gay Byrne stayed here and loved it. *Trail-riding for 3 or 4 hours a day for about £12 an hour.*

Rooms: 8: 4 doubles en suite shower; 1 twin en/s shower; 1 family and 1 triple sharing 1 bathroom and 1 shower; 1 single en/s shower.
Price: £23 — £25 p.p. Sing. supp £6.
Breakfast: Included — full Irish.
Meals: Dinner by arrangement (7 pm) £18.
Closed: Dec 20th — Dec 28th.

How to get there: Take N24 south from Limerick, direction Tipperary. 5 miles past Tipperary, entrance to Bansha signposted, turning on left. First big entrance on right opposite stand of evergreens.

Map Ref No: 12

Lismacue House

Bansha
Co. Tipperary

Tel: 062-54106
Fax: 062-54126
E-mail: lismac@indigo.ie

Katherine Nicholson

Jim, an easy-mannered barrister, presides at dinner with a stock of well-told equestrian anecdotes; he used to show-jump. The stables hold 30 racehorses in training and his wife Kate — whose family built Lismacue 200 years ago — was sitting up that night with a foaling mare. We went along after crab cakes and locally-grown T-bone to watch the filly's first steps and returned to finish our claret with the cheese. You can admire, or climb, Galtymore from here, fish in their river or ride on the 200-acre estate. The house is voluminous: high ornate ceilings, excellent furniture sparingly arranged, block-printed papers and big carpets echoing the light greens, blues and greys. Never overdone. Not sumptuous but elegant, aristocratic and graceful — cool even — except for the large and cosily cluttered drawing room with its tapestry, fireplace, lots of stuffed chairs and deep cheerful blue suite. The bedrooms are vast, light, airy with big, shuttered windows and beds afloat on seas of pale wool carpeting; and there's a smaller, darker four-poster with ancient leather chest and unique green tapestry carpet. The lime avenue deserves a mention, too.

Rooms: 5 doubles: 3 en suite; 2 sharing bathroom.
Price: £33 — £40 p.p. Sing. supp. £7.
Breakfast: Included — full Irish.
Meals: Dinner £21. Packed lunches on request.
Closed: December 20th — January 2nd.

How to get there: From Cahir take N24 towards Tipperary (12 miles). Entrance on right just before Bansha signpost at bridge. Drive up lime tree avenue to house.

Dualla House

Dualla/Kilkenny Rd
Cashel
Co. Tipperary

Tel: 062-61487
Fax: 062-61487
E-mail: duallahse@tinet.ie
www: http://ireland.iol.ie/tipp/dualla-house.htm

Mairead Power

The four children started to move out and now there's just one son left to run the farm with husband Martin. And what a farm!, an ordered lesson in sheep husbandry, visited by other farmers. Pens with different breeds (Cheviot, Suffolk...) are laid out logically for lambing, shearing etc. It's an easy, clean and safe place to walk around and there's plenty to see, with the dogs in the fields and the flowers and vegetables in the old walled kitchen garden. Inside, this 200-year-old Georgian manor house is well-proportioned and well-furnished in solid farmhouse style. There are the original polished floorboards in the breakfast room, fresh flowers and paintings from Korea brought back by her nun sister. The walls are four-foot thick and make chunky hallway arches and solid turf-burning fireplaces. The bathrooms and bedrooms are big, with orthopaedic mattresses and views over fields of sheep. The poem, Desiderata, hangs on the wall; Mairead knows it by heart. It starts, "Go quietly amidst the noise and haste and remember what peace there may be in silence". At Dualla, it is a silence full of lambs!

Rooms: 4: 2 family; 1 twin; 1 double; all en suite.
Price: £18 — £20 p.p. Sing. supp. £5 — £10.
Breakfast: Included — full Irish.
Meals: Not available.
Closed: December 1st — February 1st.

How to get there: From Cashel at top of main street turn right. Pass church on left. Take left signposted to Dualla (3 miles). Down hill, house is up in field on left — sign at gate.

115   **Map Ref No:** 12

Killaghy Castle
Mullinahone
Co. Tipperary

Tel: 052-53112

Marie and Pat Collins

The crumbling 13th-century Norman tower now has marigolds growing through its windows, but the Irish Heritage house is in tip-top shape. Pat and Marie have worked tirelessly to create a really comfortable and blissfully quiet retreat since bringing their young family from Cork two years ago. Behind the solid, red front door are a stag's head and rooms of chunky antiques, flower-filled alcoves and even a games room with pool and video for Nintendo-starved kids. Upstairs, big rose bedrooms with embossed wallpaper, black wooden floors and oak furniture lead off a wide hall and there are bay window views of the valley of Slievenamon. The Collins are ardent hosts, never more so than during the traditional summer poetry readings in the birdsong-filled walled garden with its 400-year-old forked evergreen towering above. The farmyard and Mullinahone's tennis courts are two minutes walk away, with four pubs not much further.

Rooms: 5: 2 family; 2 doubles; 1 twin: 2 with separate bathrooms, 3 en suite.
Price: £18 — £20 p.p. Sing. supp. £5.
Breakfast: Included — full Irish.
Meals: Dinner £15 (on request). High tea £9.
Closed: December 1st — March 1st.

How to get there: From Kilkenny to Callan go 0.5 miles and turn right, signposted Mullinahone. Through village. 0.5 miles from village on Ballingarry road, grey stone entrance forks off on left.

Map Ref No: 12

Lady's Abbey

Ardfinnan
Co. Tipperary

Tel: 052-66209
Fax: 052-66209
E-mail: ladysaby@iol.ie
www: http://www.iol.ie/tipp/lady's-abbey.htm

Joe and Lynda Buckley

When I visited I had to drive through a foot and a half of the flooded River Suir before climbing the hill in Ardfinnan to Lady's Abbey. But it was lovely in the middle of four days of solid rain to be sat down, cosseted with umpteen cups of tea and have a chat about the weather. Joe and Lynda are from Florida and one of the principal causes of their move was a hurricane (are they weather magnets?). They are an incredibly easy-going couple who bring a little American spice to this deeply rural corner of Ireland. Potatoes are out. Sacrilege! Instead they cook with rice, or do barbecues outside, mixing a little Floridian cuisine with Irish ingredients. They like their guests to mingle too. The house has a superb position, with flowers outside windows and apple trees in the garden. This is also a horsey place with stable yard and lunging ring. Inside, the big bedrooms are decorated in whites and creams with views over the Knockmealdown Mountains, big shower-rooms, tiled floors, ample wooden beds. Throughout the house there is a feeling of space. *There's trout fishing nearby.*

Rooms: 3: 1 family with en suite bath; 1 triple with en suite shower; 1 double with en suite shower.
Price: £20 p.p. Sing. supp. £6.50.
Breakfast: Included — full Irish.
Meals: Dinner £16.
Closed: Never!

How to get there: From Dublin N7 then N8 — follow to Cahir. There, follow sign from centre towards Ardfinnan. At T-junction turn right into Ardfinnan. Over bridge, along river, then up the hill — house signed through trees.

117

Map Ref No: 17

The South-West

Glanworth Mill

Glanworth
Fermoy
Co. Cork

Tel: 025-38555
Fax: 025-38560
E-mail: glanworth@iol.ie
www: www.iol.ie/glanworth

Lynne Glasscoe and Emelyn Heaps

I know before starting there won't be enough room here to say all there is to say about Glanworth. What a treat on all counts! Its position is the first thing to strike you — right by the River Funcheon, beside a fifteenth-century, narrow, stone-arched bridge and built into a cliff-face with an imposing Norman Castle perched like a hat above. Inside, the river turns the huge mill-wheels behind a glass wall in the tea rooms, an unusually soothing presence. The site is stupendous and has had film crews jostling for their turn. It won't go to the head of Lynne and Emelyn, though, two of the most relaxed people you'd hope to meet. This seems to have its knock-on effect, as happy-looking young staff bustle around the restaurant and tearooms. Downstairs features a library with stone fireplace and beamed mantlepiece where a piano is played on Sundays. All is bright and beautiful, great country style in everything and the writer-themed rooms are enchanting. Suffice it to say that none lack for anything — and the pièce de résistance is the Seamus Murphy room whose back wall is exposed, white-painted cliff-face.

Rooms: 10: 8 doubles with en suite bath; 2 doubles/twins with en suite bath.
Price: £35 — £38 p.p. Sing. supp £10.
Breakfast: Included — full Irish.
Meals: Dinner (6 nights/wk) in Fleece 'n' Loom à la carte. Average main course £13. Tea room bistro 10 am — 8 pm.
Closed: December 24th — 29th.

How to get there: From Dublin take N8 south — between Mitchelstown and Fermoy turn right signed Glanworth. Continue for 5 miles, over old bridge, mill under castle on right by the river.

118

Map Ref No: 17

Ballyvolane House

Castlelyons
Co. Cork

Tel: 025-36349
Fax: 025-36781
E-mail: ballyvol@iol.ie
www: http://www.iol.ie/ballyvolane/

Jeremy and Merrie Green

If you tell anyone in southern Ireland that you're staying at Ballyvolane that night you will get a nod of approval. This is one of Ireland's best old houses, furnished with much grace and taste, luxuriously comfortable, run by extremely humorous, easy-going people and surrounded by one of Ireland's most stunning private gardens. High ceilings loom over the large columned hall with its piano that talented guests are encouraged to play, over the vast dining room where mock Egyptian lucifers stand attendant during dinner parties, and over the kitchen, which is the size of a small house. Upstairs all is luxury — grand bedrooms lie off a long narrow corridor, each different, with beds like comfortable football pitches; there are antique dressers and wardrobes, thick carpets, tall windows, armchairs designed to be sat upon. If you don't have that room, do try and see the amazing early 19th-century bath. The Greens utterly deserve their reputation and are very popular with anglers. Merrie will organise fishing if asked.

Rooms: 6: 2 doubles en suite; 1 double with adjacent bathroom; 2 twins with en suite bath; 1 twin with adjacent bath.
Price: £35 — £45 p.p. Sing. supp. £10.
Breakfast: Included — full Irish.
Meals: Dinner £23. Packed lunches for fishermen £5.
Closed: December 22nd- 28th.

How to get there: From Cork N8, right onto Tallow road before Rathcormac. Follow 4 signs from Tallow turn-off.

Map Ref No: 17

Conna House

Conna
Co. Cork

Tel: 058-59419

Michael and Maura Verling

There are no regulations here. The emphasis is on a relaxed homely atmosphere, so no part of the house is blocked off to guests ('Oh, except our bedroom.'). Four good-sized rooms share exactly the same features: large single beds which convert into doubles, high pink bedsteads, workmanlike en suite showers, views over green hills and even some unlikely palms nearer to home. Blue patterned carpets lead downstairs to the sitting room which leads into the dining room through a large arch. It is here that Maura serves the home-made meals that had one group of Italians applauding at the end — 'I love feeding people,' she says. This is fishing and horse country: guests can go riding, hunting and point-to-pointing and the house is within casting distance of the River Bride.

Rooms: 4: all twin/double with en suite shower.
Price: £25 p.p. Sing. supp. £5 when busy.
Breakfast: Included — full Irish.
Meals: Dinner £25 (BYO wine). Packed lunches for fishermen £5.
Closed: Never!

How to get there: From Cork take N8 (Dublin Rd). Before village of Rathcormack turn right signed Conna, follow straight for 8 miles, house signed on right before village.

Map Ref No: 17

Ballymakeigh House

Killeagh
Youghal
Co. Cork

Tel: 024-95184
Fax: 024-95370
E-mail: ballymakeigh@tinet.ie

Margaret and Michael Browne

Margaret Browne is the 'Irish housewife of the year' who does the 'Irish breakfast of the year' — and every other meal she magics (she really does hold both these titles). The 300-year-old house in which these feasts appear is kept immaculate, warm and in perfect working order, with unexpected bonuses such as good-sized power showers. Under foot, thick patterned carpets support large, comfortable beds and views on one side are over fields. Although you can make out a road in the distance the general feeling is of great tranquillity with the farm cattle and rooks providing the background music. Downstairs there is a lovely long conservatory with pot plants and wooden furniture. But it is Margaret and her cooking that any description of Ballymakeigh must come back to. She has written a cookery book and appears regularly on TV as a chef. Ingredients are the very freshest and nearly all come from the farm. *Margaret's latest ventures are an equestrian centre and a restaurant which have just opened.*

Rooms: 5: 1 family; 4 twins/doubles: all with en suite shower or bath.
Price: £30 p.p. High season sing. supp. £10.
Breakfast: Included — full Irish.
Meals: Dinner £22.50 — £25. Wine list from £10.
Closed: November 1st — February 1st.

How to get there: Take N25 Youghal — Cork road signed 5 miles out of Youghal to right. Follow signs to Ballymakeigh House (right and right again). Tarmac drive.

Map Ref No: 17

Spanish Point Seafood Restaurant & Guest Accommodation

Ballycotton
Co. Cork

Tel: 021-646177
Fax: 021-646179

John and Mary Tattan

Mary is relaxed, very down-to-earth, easy to talk to (too easy in my case as I'm sure I should have been elsewhere by 3pm!) and cooks wonderfully. This seafood restaurant with rooms stares straight out to sea from a great height. You can see the clouds rolling in from the Atlantic, casting their shadow over the lighthouse island just off shore as you eat in the large conservatory section of the restaurant. All the fish comes fresh from John's trawler which can be seen parked by the jetties of this sweet little fishing village. "It's the only black lighthouse in Ireland!", Mary says with a slight lack of confidence. "Is that a good thing?" Rooms upstairs are all identical with low double beds, pink carpets and two of them have the view. This place is for foodies who want to eat the freshest possible seafood in an unpretentious atmosphere and mull on the larger issues of life as they gaze out to sea.

Rooms: 5: 3 double; 2 family: all with en suite shower.
Price: £25 p.p. Sing. supp. £5.
Breakfast: Included — full Irish.
Meals: Dinner £21, lunch £12, packed lunch from £5.
Closed: January 1st — Feruary 14th.

How to get there: From Cork towards Youghal (N25). Turn right in Midleton signed to Cloyne/Shanagarry/Ballycotton. In Ballycotton big sign on left.

Map Ref No: 17

Old Parochial House

Castlemartyr
Midleton
Co. Cork

Tel: 021-667454
Fax: 021-667429
E-mail: ect@tinet.ie

Paul and Kathy Sheehy

Whether as home to the local priest or bawdy casino, Old Parochial has always been an important focal point for the local community since its construction in 1784! So there was a sigh of communal relief when it was bought by locally-connected folk who refurbished it for real comfort while preserving the character of the house (I mean the building itself not its earlier functions!). Not a moment too soon, either, as nothing had been done for a hundred years. The drawing room today has deep sofas and armchairs that grab you and don't let go, floor-to-ceiling windows, a lovely fireplace, wood floors, cornicing that Paul recovered painstakingly with a toothpick, and brand new sound-proofed and cold-tight sash windows. You can sit out among the tomato plants and grape vines of the conservatory when it's warm enough. By the time I saw the bedrooms I knew I must expect great quality: a four-poster in one room, a big brass bed in another, thick carpets, sparkling bathrooms, plenty of space... Kathy and Paul are a relaxed, easy-to-get-on-with young couple who, justifiably, take pride in all aspects of their brand new enterprise.

Rooms: 3: 2 doubles with en suite bath; 1 twin/double with en suite shower.
Price: £30 — £40 p.p. No sing. supp.
Breakfast: Included — full Irish.
Meals: Spanish Point for seafood and The Clean Slate in Midleton are excellent.
Closed: December 30th — January 3rd.

How to get there: From Cork take N25 towards Waterford, bypassing Midleton. Next village Castlemartyr. Cross bridge, then immediately right signed Shanagarry, then keep immediately left. House first on left.

Glenview House

Midleton
Co. Cork

Tel: 021-631680
Fax: 021-631680

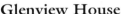

Ken and Beth Sherrard

The views are quite stunning. A low wall in front of the house entices you to look over — and from this enchanted spot you can see the lawns disappear downhill in a diving wedge of pines to an unseen river whose rushing sound demands further investigation. Across the water the valley rises again in a huge sweep of larches and forestry pines. Seclusion, peace and quiet, birds, horses, sheep — a rural idyll that is a complete surprise so close to Midleton. Bedrooms are very large with spectacular views, as many as three tall windows, 49 square feet of bed and long mirrors. And one room has a wonderful turn-of-the-century, Heath-Robinson-like, brass shower. Behind all this are Ken and Beth whose enthusiasm for entertaining shines through. Naturally they are proud of their home, but equally important are the friends they have made along the way, many of whom will go nowhere else in Ireland. This is a friendly house with bags to do: fishing on the river, riding nearby, lawn tennis, wonderful woodland walks — all in a superb position. *Two lovely self-catering cottages now available with all mod cons. Only guide dogs.*

Rooms: 4: 1 twin and 1 twin/double (wheelchair accessible) with en suite bathroom downstairs; 2 doubles.
Price: £35 — £40 p.p.
Breakfast: Included — full Irish.
Meals: Dinner £20. Please book by noon on day of arrival.
Closed: Never!

How to get there: Drive into Midleton. Do not take by-pass. At large roundabout take signs to Fermoy (L35). After 2.5 miles take L signed Leamlara in forestry area and then immediately R. Follow sign to Glenview; first entrance on L at top of hill.

Map Ref No: 17

Allcorn's Country Home

Shournagh Rd
Blarney
Co. Cork

Tel: 021-385577
Fax: 021-382828

Helen Allcorn

On a crisp, frost-white morning Helen Allcorn's wooden house reminded me of those Christmas cartoon houses that blaze an orange glow through snow-bound windows. It made me want to pad around in thick socks. The house even smells cosy! Helen built it herself 13 years ago, enchanted by the position in a wooded valley by a river, and her guests today benefit from her simple philosophy of doing-as-you-would-be-done-by (to borrow briefly from the Water Babies!). It's modern and extremely comfortable, with the sound of the River Shournagh an ever-present gurgle in the background. Helen loves animals and people alike, and her pets are often strays needing refuge. There are polished wooden floors, country baskets, rugs, flowers, wood-burning stoves — all is fresh and pretty in pine. And it was really a credit to the house's insulation on such a bitter morning that it was so warm inside. The bedrooms upstairs are equally pretty, with plenty of shower space and Egyptian cotton on beds. Breakfasts are a treat you should save time for and I recommend Helen to you wholeheartedly.

Rooms: 4: 3 doubles with en suite shower; 1 single with private bath and shower.
Price: £18 p.p. Sing. supp £7.
Breakfast: Included — full Irish.
Meals: Nearby Blair's is excellent.
Closed: End October — end March.

How to get there: From Blarney take Killarney Rd (R617) for 1 mile out of town — take first major turn to right by River Shournagh. House second on left. 'Allcorn's Country Home' is on the sign by the junction.

Map Ref No: 17

Maranatha Country House

Tower
Blarney
Co. Cork

Tel: 021-385102
Fax: 021-385102
cork-guide.ie/blarney/maranatha/welcome.html

Olwen and Douglas Venn

Olwen has created an extraordinary place to stay. Every room astonishes; they are so utterly different that it takes time to adjust from one to another. They are fantasies centred round large, ornate beds, sometimes four-poster, sometimes king-size. One room is like a flower garden, another like a cool forest; the next features a regal-style bed with a velvet crown supported on a wine-coloured velvet-draped frame, the deep burgundies, pinks and reds refreshed by real lilacs. You have to see them to believe them. One room has over 400 yards of material in its draperies. Olwen is enormously enthusiastic about the house and shows great daring in her designs. Eating here is an experience too. Wonderful breakfasts are taken in a flower-filled conservatory that again you could not possibly imagine. And the whole house is secluded on a hill surrounded by wonderful monkey-puzzle and rhododendrons and specially designed walks through the woods. At the prices she and Douglas are charging this is a special place indeed.

Rooms: 6: 3 doubles/family, 1 en/s bath, 2 en/s shower; 1 double en/s sh; 1 family en/s sh; 1 double en/s bath.
Price: £19 — £25 p.p. Regal suite with whirlpool — £30.
Breakfast: Included — full Irish.
Meals: Several excellent restaurants nearby.
Closed: 1st week November — end of March.

How to get there: From Cork take N20 towards Blarney. Through village, and after 1.5 miles signed up hill to right just after sign entering Tower.

Map Ref No: 17

D'Arcy's

7 Sidney Place
Wellington Rd, Cork
Co. Cork

Tel: 021-504658/504522
Fax: 021-502-791

Clare D'Arcy

Not until you enter D'Arcy's do you realize what a large building this is. Built in 1810 for Murphys the brewery people (Clare thinks), it has ceilings and rooms that seem immeasurable, becoming lower and smaller as the house rises. And rise it does! Clare jokes that she doesn't charge for the step aerobics; it's 92 stairs from the kitchen and breakfast room in the basement. En route you pass lush green plants and pictures by Clare's daughter. Breakfast is freshly squeezed, freshly ground, freshly baked with hot porridge and cream and home-made preserves. The family is scattered among the many rooms in the house. All the walls have recently been repainted in very bold bright yellows, mauves, pinks and reds and massive bedrooms have outstanding views over the city, the higher the better. The rooms are uncluttered, calm, cool places, very peaceful right in the centre of such a hectic city. And Clare herself brims with good humour. She seems to know all her guests as friends.

Rooms: 6: all double: 2 with en suite shower; 4 sharing 2 showers, 1 bath and 2 toilets.
Price: £25 — £27.50 p.p. £25 for singles for '99.
Breakfast: Included — full Irish.
Meals: Available locally.
Closed: Christmas Eve and Day.

How to get there: In Cork City centre. Ask when booking.

Map Ref No: 17

Tracton House Abbey

Tracton, Minane Bridge
Carigaline
Co. Cork

Tel: 021-887310
Fax: 021-887310

Bob and Maura Carpenter

At first glance Tracton House is just another early nineteenth-century country church. But this is a most unusual place to stay, a treasure for this book. The surprises keep coming. The interior has been lovingly restored with impeccable taste by its down-to-earth and irrepressibly gregarious owners, Bob and Maura. The result is a two-storey structure within the original shell and the atmosphere is that of a medieval castle. The fabulous state-of-the-art conversion has earned it great publicity including seven pages in House and Home magazine. There is Tudor pannelling which blends with mahogany, dark-stained timbers in the hall, and the old church organ and bell remain. Bedrooms are gorgeous, several of them boasting headboards transmogrified from old carved altar timbers; and bathrooms are pristine, beautifully tiled, with power showers and at least one old-fashioned free-standing bath. One of the bathroom doors was once an old confessional door. Historic Kinsale and the Carpenters' excellent restaurant Annalies are nearby.

Rooms: 6: 1 twin with en/s bath; 1 single with en/s shower; 2 doubles en/s shower; 2 doubles sharing 1 bath.
Price: £25 — £30 p.p. Single £30. Sing. supp. for double or twin £5.
Breakfast: Included — full Irish.
Meals: They own Annalies Restaurant in Kinsale, but also a very good pub across the way.
Closed: November 12th — March 16th.

How to get there: Follow Ringaskiddy Ferry signs (N28) to roundabout. Drive to Carigaline, thro' village, turn right onto Kinsale Rd R611. At Ballyfeard turn left, 0.5 km to Overdraught Bar. Tracton House is opposite on right.

Map Ref No: 17

Ducey House
Denis Quay
Kinsale
Co. Cork

Tel: 021-774592

Helen Whitley

Helen was an ideal person to set up her own B&B. She has a warm personality, she's a Ballymaloe-trained cook — she was a chef at Temple House in Sligo which is also in this book — and she's an artist with a flair for interiors. Ducey House (Queen Anne, a rarity in Ireland but fairly common in historic Kinsale) is found tucked into the corner of its very attractive gravelled courtyard right by the harbour waters. Park your car outside the house. I visited in winter and the place exuded warmth and homeliness — a real fire blazed in the low-ceilinged drawing room. Helen has painted the floorboards on the staircase and her pictures are on the walls too. The rooms are sweet, with old doors and shuttered windows, angled windows in the eaves, thick red carpets or wooden floors, rows of sash windows that look onto the harbour, the odd marble fireplace and there is one lovely bathroom with free-standing bath AND shower. Light floods into the rooms in the morning. This is a cosy old house where food is wonderful and the welcome genuine from both Helen and her red setter.

Rooms: 4: 2 doubles, 1 family and 1 twin; 1 with en suite bath, 3 with en suite shower.
Price: £18 — £25 p.p. Sing supp £5 — £8. Winter house parties for groups £60 — £80 weekend incl' 2 dinners.
Breakfast: Included — full Irish.
Meals: Dinner for groups by arrangement: £20 (4 courses).
Closed: A three-week break some time in early spring.

How to get there: From Cork into Kinsale, left at Post Office. Follow road round harbour to left. First turn to right after Acton's Hotel, house off road to right.

Map Ref No: 17

Sovereign House

Kinsale
Co. Cork

Tel: 021-772850
Fax: 021-774723

James McKeown

The Sovereign of Kinsale was a position akin to mayor and two of them have lived in this stunning Queen Anne townhouse (1706). You'll find it down the twisting narrow back streets, a suitably dignified residence. There's an almost Gothic flavour to the place with a cool, moody atmosphere born of classical music, 300-year-old doors, beamed ceilings, carved high-back chairs, dark woods and exposed stone. But dashes of contrasting modern art lighten the tone. James is obviously a man of diverse talents. A diver by profession he also clearly has an eye for fine things. Upstairs, behind pannelled doors, everything is designed for your comfort. One huge room has been set aside for a full-size snooker table. The others are bedrooms. All have their own Victorian bathroom with free-standing bath and wood-mounted washbasins. Bathrobes are provided for lounging on high four-poster beds. There's modern luxury to attend your every whim. Breakfasts are another source of pride with unusual extras including smoked salmon, goat's cheese and apple tarts.

Rooms: 4: 3 four-posters and 1 four poster PLUS extra single; 3 with en suite bath; 1 with en suite shower.
Price: £50 — £65 p.p. Sing. supp. £15.
Breakfast: Included — full Irish.
Meals: Good restaurants abound.
Closed: Christmas.

How to get there: From Cork into Kinsale, straight on at Post Office, right at White House Hotel. Next sharp left, house on right.

Map Ref No: 17

The Old Presbytery
43 Cork St
Kinsale
Co. Cork

Tel: 021-772027
oldpres@iol.ie
www: wwwoldpres.ie

Philip and Noreen McEvoy

Kinsale is a popular and attractive little fishing town within easy striking distance of Cork and its airport. And The Old Presbytery is hidden away in the bewildering maze of backstreets. The old part of the house was built in the 1780s and your hosts have managed to create modern comfort while respecting the house's age. This part remains the same as last year. Elsewhere Philip and Noreen have worked wonders. It's still very much a guesthouse, not a hotel, and Philip's breakfasts are a priority. They have converted and adjoined the next-door house and the new rooms are every bit as appealing as the originals — great ingenuity and intriguing design have been brought to bear. The most interesting room has a spiral staircase in the middle of it that leads up to another sleeping area. You can lift the downstairs bed into the wall and have a sitting room. This sort of flexibility means you can self-cater here too. Rooms have big baths with Victorian-style basin units, pine furniture — one double room has a whirlpool bath. Views are across Kinsale's lovely roofscape and out to Charles Fort.

9: 3 self-catering apartments sleeping 6; 5 doubles/twins and 1 family, all with en suite bath or shower.
Price: £25 — £35 p.p. Sing. supp. £10. 3 double suites sleeping 4/6 @ £180 per night.
Breakfast: Included — full Irish.
Meals: Kinsale is the 'gourmet capital of Ireland'!
Closed: Never!

How to get there: From Cork take N28 to airport, follow signs to Kinsale. In Kinsale do not follow road round to left but continue straight down Pearse St. Left at junction, 1st right, 1st right again. House 1st on right.

Map Ref No: 17

131

The Lighthouse
Kinsale
Co. Cork

Tel: 021-772734
Fax: 021-773282 or 774206
E-mail: reservations@corkwideweb.com
www: www.corkwideweb.com/lighthousekinsale

Carmel Kelly-O'Gorman

Carmel will whisk you into her domain with breathless enthusiasm. She's a great talker and laugher, indulging in typical "Irish arabesque conversation". The house stands on the site of an old lighthouse. Her rooms are small and feminine with a lot of pinks, lace bedhead drapes, chocolates placed on the bed etc — some quite rare items of Irish lace are flattened beneath glass-topped bedside tables. This is a particular interest of Carmel's who embroiders her own sheets. The quilts are all hand-made too, hand-me-downs from her family. Each room has been given a theme which is lightly adhered to. The Out of Africa room, for example, has a lace mosquito net and two small David Shepherd paintings on the wall. Shower-rooms are adequately contrived from existing room space. Carmel is a traveller so the whole house is dotted with bits and bobs from Asia and Africa. The Lighthouse has an atmosphere born of Carmel's enthusiasm. The *Sunday Telegraph*, by the way, said that Carmel's breakfasts are as good as in any five-star hotel and the menu as varied and extensive.

Rooms: 6: 1 twin, 4 doubles and 1 suite, all with en suite shower.
Price: £20 — £30 p.p. Sing. supp £20 — £30.
Breakfast: Included — full Irish.
Meals: Kinsale has 49 restaurants.
Closed: Never!

How to get there: From Cork into Kinsale, straight on by Post Office, left at White House Hotel. Wiggle along road until signed right to Bandon. Right here, up hill. House on right.

The Gallery
The Glen
Kinsale
Co. Cork

Tel: 021-774558

Carole and Tom O'Hare

The Gallery is a one-off sort of place, very friendly, small and personal. Tom is a jazz musician and music teacher and the bright breakfast area gently wafts jazz across you as you eat. On jazz nights Tom sits down to his vibraphone or piano and there are also plans for informal, lunch-time, classical recitals with wine — they have a licence. Carole complements the artistic theme as a very accomplished painter and all the pictures on the walls at the Gallery are hers. This is an informal home with five smallish rooms upstairs that have seagrass matting floors, white walls and wooden beds. The O'Haras have put in TVs too and you can make yourself tea or coffee. To the rear the house looks onto the old lighthouse left over from the days when the road there was a waterway. Quite a lot of Kinsale has been reclaimed from the old wharves and docks — Tom will fill you in. He's a mine of information on this historic town.

Rooms: 5: 1 family and 4 doubles, all with en suite shower.
Price: £20 — £30 p.p. Sing. supp £0 — £10.
Breakfast: Included — full Irish.
Meals: Evening meals from £10 — £15 July — September.
Closed: Christmas.

How to get there: From Cork into Kinsale, straight on at Post Office, right at White House Hotel, 50 yards on left.

Leighmoneymore
Dunderrow
Kinsale
Co. Cork

Tel: 021-775312
Fax: 021-775692

Dominique O'Sullivan-Vervaet

This 1912 farmhouse (built as a dowry) has the most lovely position in a most lovely area — right by the sea among hills and tiny lanes and close to Kinsale with its great variety of excellent eateries. At the bottom of their land, past the newly planted forestry, is a secluded sea inlet, banked by hills on all sides. Leighmoneymore keeps a jetty and boat there. The River Bandon also runs through their property. Dominique (Dutch, English, French, Italian, Spanish and German-speaking) runs the B&B side of things, very informal and friendly. There was a great feeling of life about the place, with cows in the field and children playing outside. Breakfasts are taken on wicker chairs in the new conservatory, while the sitting room in the older part of the house has wood floors, green plants, furniture you're not afraid to sit in and shallow bay windows looking onto the garden. Upstairs, the bedrooms have long views and lots of space. They have recently completed a new annexe, keeping to the style of the old house. Polished wooden floors gleam and there are big brass beds and proper large bathrooms. Wonderful seclusion.

Rooms: 5: 3 doubles with en suite bath; 2 double/twins with en suite shower.
Price: £20 — £25 p.p. Sing. supp. £10.
Breakfast: Included — full Irish.
Meals: Available in Kinsale, 'gourmet capital of the south'.
Closed: November 1st — March 15th.

How to get there: From Cork take N71 towards Innishannon. In Innishannon take R605 towards Kinsale, past Innishannon House Hotel — 3.5 miles further signpost to house on right.

Map Ref No: 17

Assolas Country House

Kanturk
Co. Cork

Tel: 029-50015
Fax: 029-50795
E-mail: assolas@tinet.ie
www: www.assolas.com

Joe and Hazel Bourke

Not many hotels appeal to me in Ireland. Many are well run, many have excellent facilities, but few have that personal touch that sets them apart. Assolas is one such place. Joe and Hazel are an unflustered, unflappable young couple and they run this country house as a family affair. The laid-back veneer may encourage guests to slump in deep armchairs by the roaring log fire — but behind the scenes the Bourkes take great pride in the staff training they provide. So service is exemplary, by which I mean right for the style of the house — friendly, helpful and proficient. Food is excellent too (fruit and veg from the walled garden). The house itself is Queen Anne (1740) with rounded ends, so some of the larger bedrooms have great sweeping curved walls. You can choose rooms in the house (which I prefer) or in the courtyard which are even quieter. Views on one side of the house are over the River Owenbeg, a Blackwater tributary, that was beautifully landscaped into the garden in the 1700s. All the rooms are of a high standard, as you'd expect, and this is a little-visited, horse-mad area of Ireland.

Rooms: 9: 3 courtyard standards en/s bath; 3 superiors and 3 standards in the house with en/s bath and shower.
Price: £55 – £83 p.p. Sing. supp £10 – £15.
Breakfast: Included — full Irish.
Meals: Dinner £32.
Closed: November 1st — March 25th.

How to get there: From Mallow take N72 towards Killarney — 8 miles west turn right towards Kanturk. After 1 mile house signed to right. Follow signs to house.

Glenlohane

Kanturk
Co. Cork

Tel: 029-50014
Fax: 029-51100

Desmond and Melanie Sharp Bolster

The Sharp and Bolster clans are spread thickly over this region where they have been rooted in the North Cork soil for several hundred years. Lovely Glenlohane was built by an ancestor in 1741 and it has remained with the family ever since. Desmond returned to the fold, after many years in America, with Melanie, who is American but espouses — and is espoused by — all that is Irish. They are great characters, full of anecdote and humour... so easy to settle in here. The house is on 300 acres, surrounded by sheep fields, horse paddocks, parkland and in the distance Mount Hilary. Animals play a big role at the house. Apart from the livestock, Desmond keeps hunters in a field, his hens are like pets... and Melanie takes in mistreated and unwanted greyhounds. There are many, many dogs. Nature and wildlife seem to bloom here where the countryside is held in such high esteem. Inside, antiques grace elegant yet informal rooms and bedrooms are clean, fresh, bright, multi-windowed, large, with a 4-poster in one case and proper bathrooms in all but one case. A very special place to stay for great fun and great comfort.

Rooms: 5: 2 doubles and 3 twins, all with private bath and/or shower.
Price: £45 — £50 p.p. Sing. supp. £10.
Breakfast: Included — full Irish.
Meals: Dinner £25 (not on Sundays).
Closed: Never!

How to get there: From Kanturk take R576 towards Mallow. Bear left on R580 towards Buttevant. First right towards Ballyclough, first entrance on left after 2.5 km — signed 'Glenlohane Bird Sanctuary'.

Map Ref No: 16

Kilbrittain Castle

Kilbrittain
Co. Cork

Tel: 023-49601
Fax: 023-49702
E-mail: timcob@iol.ie

Tim and Sylvia Cahill-O'Brien

Here's a rare opportunity to stay in a medieval castle. Originally built in 1035, it has since been occupied by Irish chieftains, Norman invaders, Cromwellian troops and Anglo-Norman planters. It is now an Irish family home in grand surroundings. Sweep down and up the parabola of the drive, past the Irish setters at the gate, to the forbidding stone façade and its wonderful external double staircase. The steps are uneven to make life difficult for invaders so today's approach is via a huge sturdy door and a spiral staircase, whence you emerge in a long, stone-floored gallery. From the guests' dining room, with its welcoming fire, two lovely old leaded windows look over a wooded valley and estuary. Upstairs, dark wood beams and thick doors guard modern beds and bathrooms. Scattered about the main castle are a number of innovations — weights for shutting heavy doors gently, hidden light switches, vestiges of the house's previous owners. Fishing, tennis, scuba-diving, sailboarding and sailing available nearby. Also unique golfing holidays. *No children under 3 years.*

Rooms: 5: 2 doubles and 3 family, all with bath and shower.
Price: £40 p.p. 50% discount for children under 12 sharing parents' bedroom. Sing. supp. £8.
Breakfast: Included — full Irish.
Meals: Available locally in excellent restaurants.
Closed: October 31st — May 1st.

How to get there: From Cork take N71 to Bandon, then R603 to Kilbrittain (6 miles). Signed in village.

Travara Lodge

Courtmacsherry
Co. Cork

Tel: 023-46493
Fax: 023-46045
E-mail: travara@tinet.ie

Marie and Damien Enright

Travara is an unelaborate 1820s gentleman's residence right by the water with nice wooden windows and views. The sitting room is thickly carpeted and rugged with bureau bookcase, large hunting table and very comfortable sofa and chairs in white woven cotton, while bedrooms are unfussy but warm. The area is criss-crossed with sea inlets, causeways, hills — and Courtmacsherry in particular is a walker's paradise backing onto the Earl of Shannon's estate. The woodland walks have you patrolling the wild coastal coves until you stand on the heads looking out over clear Atlantic. And it remains a fairly unknown enclave... except to birds, that is. Thousands flock here and no-one is in a better position to help guests with advice on species, binoculars and where to go than Damien; he is an infectiously enthusiastic talker, nature writer and radio broadcaster. Both he and Marie create a chatty, bustling, fun atmosphere. This is a down-to-earth family home in a wonderful spot. Fresh-water and deep-sea angling are a major feature of Courtmacsherry. Breakfasts are a speciality too.

Rooms: 6: 4 doubles/twins; 2 family/doubles/twins; 5 with en suite shower, 1 with en suite bath and shower.
Price: £18 — £20 p.p. Sing. supp. £5.
Breakfast: Included — full Irish and other choices.
Meals: Good restaurants in village and in Timoleague.
Closed: November 4th — March 14th.

How to get there: From Cork take R71 to Bandon, on to Timoleague, signed to Courtmacsherry; house on right.

Map Ref No: 16

Lettercollum House

Timoleague
Co. Cork

Tel: 023-46251
Fax: 023-46270
E-mail: conmc@iol.ie
www: http://www.clon.ie/letterco.html

Con McLoughlin and Karen Austin

One of Ireland's most idiosyncratic places to stay and eat, this large Victorian mansion used to be a convent and has developed organically under the back-to-nature creativity of Con and Karen. The talents of friends and visitors have been put to great use here — a few have never left and are still living in the converted stable block. The results are maverick, of high quality, relaxed and great fun. Rooms are huge and with fine views, some over the water at Timoleague. On the night I stayed there was an unlikely and very effective production of Aeschylus's 'The Persians' (!) performed by a Japanese lady and an Englishman in the drawing room. The audience then ate a wonderful meal in the candlelit restaurant (a great favourite locally) where the conviviality was testament to the atmosphere at Lettercollum. All the produce comes from a huge walled garden and staff are young and friendly. The interior is in bold and bright colours and a huge arched stained window illuminates the staircase. Perfect for families who can cook for their kids, put them to bed and return to the restaurant. *The whole house is available for self-catering Dec-Feb.*

Rooms: 9: all doubles: 8 with en/s shower; 1 with en/s bath.
Price: £20 — £30 p.p. Sing. supp. £6 — £10.
Breakfast: Included — full Irish.
Meals: Dinner £21.50, lunch £12. (Kitchen area available.)
Closed: January and February. November weekends only.

How to get there: From Cork take N71 to Bandon, then R602 to Timoleague. In town go through the village onto Clonakilty Rd, up a hill, signed to right.

Butlerstown House

Butlerstown, Timoleague
Bandon
Co. Cork

Tel: 023-40137 mob: 087-2203672
Fax: 023-40137

Elisabeth Jones and Roger Owen

Lis Jones and Roger Owen have recently taken over this fine Georgian house, and as Roger is an antiques restorer, no doubt they'll continue to add to its already wonderful array of furniture. But there's no need to fear that it might become too grand and intimidating because Lis and Roger are a relaxed, friendly Welsh couple who laugh a lot and make their guests feel instantly at home. The proportions of the house are perfect — elegant staircase and large airy rooms with incredible cornices. Big windows give extensive views across fields to the sea. Four-poster beds, a Regency sideboard and a 14-foot mahogany dining table complement the architectural features, but log fires, candlelit dinners (off-season), a brand new power hot water system, and a massive but homely kitchen ensure it also retains the warmth and ambience of an informal country house. Breakfasts are gourmet affairs. As well as a very full Irish spread, the laverbread, cockles, wild Ummera smoked salmon, smoked haddock and Castletownbere kippers are worth special mention. This house is a treat and one of my favourites in this area of Ireland. *Children over 12 years welcome.*

Rooms: 4: 2 doubles and 2 twins: 1 with en suite shower; 2 with en suite bath; 1 with private shower.
Price: £35 — £55 p.p. (dependent on season and length of stay). No sing. supp.
Breakfast: Included — full Irish/Celtic.
Meals: Dinners by arrangement off season only. A wide choice nearby.
Closed: Never!

How to get there: From Cork take N71 to Bandon, then R602 to Timoleague, then Barryroe, then Butlerstown. House signed to right as you approach village.

140   Map Ref No: 16

The Castle

Castletownshend
Nr Skibbereen
Co. Cork

Tel: 028 36100
Fax: 028 36166

Anne and Malcolm Cochrane-Townshend

Castletownshend grew up around the eponymous family who have lived in the castle since it was built in the 1700s. And what a lovely village! It dives downhill past the trees in the road to where the castle basks by the sea. Artists have always been attracted to this spot; most famously it was home to the writing partnership of Somerville and Ross, authors of the Irish RM. The castle has been welcoming guests for over 50 years. Take breakfast, looking out to sea, in the grand dining room which brims with antiques, portraits and original furnishings. Elsewhere, the dark panelling and more antique furniture are absolutely in keeping with the castle. Bedrooms, meanwhile, are full of old-style curios and antiques and have wonderful views: one has a crenellated balcony; there's a 4-poster, old leather chairs. This is hard to beat. For dinner try famous Mary Ann's pub up the road, open since the 1800s.

Rooms: 7: 5 doubles with en suite bathroom; 1 double with private bathroom; 1 single with private bathroom.
Price: £25 — £45 p.p.
Breakfast: Included — full Irish.
Meals: Mary Ann's in the village has a full restaurant upstairs and bar food downstairs.
Closed: December 15th — January 10th.

How to get there: From Cork take N71 to Skibbereen, signed to Castletownshend. Down the hill; castle at the end by the water.

Map Ref No: 16

Baltimore Bay

Baltimore
Co. Cork

Tel: 028-20136 *RESTAURANT*
or try 20441

Youen Jacob

There are two Youen Jacobs here. The elder sailed from Brittany 30 years ago and never returned. He looks as though he may have spent much of that time at sea, too, with a big beard and a gruff but warm eccentricity. Youen Junior's mother (a schoolteacher) is from nearby Sherkin Island and the family business has centred around Youen's two restaurants; wonderful seafood at Chez Youen and steaks at La Jolie Brise. A couple of doors away is the Jacobs' most recent venture, the guesthouse. It was originally built in 1850, but they have remained faithful to the original look of the house by retaining the façade and reusing the old slates. Rooms have pieces of period furniture, modern and comfortable beds and five have the sea view; the others look to the rear over the garden. Baltimore Bay is a charming little fishing port running ferries over to the islands of Clear and Sherkin. Youen junior organises sailing lessons, boat charters, horse-riding and sea fishing. Baltimore is what you want from an old Irish fishing village; views, seafood, boats and traditional music... and above all the sea itself.

Rooms: 8: 3 doubles; 4 triples; 1 for the disabled.
Price: £32.50 p.p.
Breakfast: Included — full Irish.
Meals: £10 in La Jolie Brise; £18 at Chez Youen.
Closed: Never!

How to get there: From Cork take N71 to Skibbereen — signed to Baltimore. On the square in Baltimore.

Map Ref No: 16

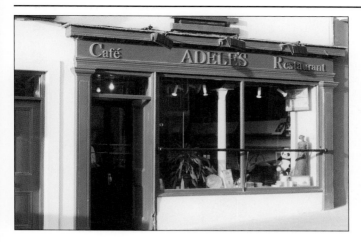

Adèle's

Main Street
Schull
Co. Cork

Tel: 028-28459
Fax: 028-28865

Adèle and Simon Connor

This little café/restaurant/B&B has a charm of its own. It sits in the middle of Schull which itself sits in the stunning scenic region of West Cork. There is the smell of freshly-baked bread hovering around the pitch-pine tables, staircase and red candles. Food is all baked on the premises (no additives). Adèle is in just the right business (from a customer's point of view!). She is easy, smiley, humorous; the unfussy, relaxed atmosphere of her establishment tells you so. Up the little staircase are three small rooms with dark wood floors and doors, sweet little windows and windowboxes. One room has an unexpected view of Clear and Sherkin Islands off nearby Baltimore. Only one shower services all these rooms but downstairs there is a bath. Be careful not to follow the example of one guest: the café filled up while he was in the bath and he had to run the gauntlet, dressed only in a towel, back to the safety of his room. Schull is a cosmopolitan place (there's even a planetarium) and is a honeypot for walkers, anglers and sailing enthusiasts.

Rooms: 3: 2 twins and 1 double sharing 1 shower room.
Price: £14.50 p.p. No sing. supp.
Breakfast: Included — Continental.
Meals: Dinner £10 — £15, lunch £5.
Closed: November 1st — December 21st and January 4th — Easter.

How to get there: From Cork N71 to Ballydehob. Follow sign to Schull — Adèle's in centre of village.

Map Ref No: 16

143

The Heron's Cove

Goleen
Co. Cork

Tel: 028-35225
Fax: 028-35422
E-mail: suehill@tinet.ie
www: westcorkweb.ie

Sue Hill

This is a spectacular part of Ireland with its deep inlets, steepling cliffs, seas that either flash with scintillas of sunlight or thunder and crash against the rocky headlands. The roads of the region dip, plunge, twist, climb, clamber round the hills, sometimes petering out, sometimes leading to beach or village — an explorer's heaven. And the Heron's Cove is the perfect base for the region. Sitting right on its own bay, it has rooms that all have lovely views, lots of window, lots of light. There is a balcony with wide-armed wooden chairs, a wonderful place to sit out on warm days and shared by several rooms. Downstairs is the heart of the house, a large, airy restaurant room with a fire at each end, wicker chairs and a wine rack with up to 60 wines to choose from. Sue is relaxed and easy with her guests — who tend to come back — and food here is fresh and delicious. As the brochure has it, "Fresh fish and wine on the harbour".

Rooms: 5: 1 double with en suite bath; 2 doubles/triples and 2 twins/singles with en suite showers.
Price: £18.50 — £25 p.p. Double with extra single £62. Single £25 — £31.50.
Breakfast: Included — full Irish.
Meals: Dinner £19.50. A la carte from 12 to 9.45 pm. Restaurant open from May — October.
Closed: Christmas week.

How to get there: From Cork take N71 to Ballydehob, then signed to Schull, then signed to Goleen — turn left down narrow turning to the harbour.

Map Ref No: 15

Rock Cottage

Barnatonicane
Nr Schull
Co. Cork

Tel: 028-35538
Fax: 028-35538

Barbara Klötzer

Barbara is a no-nonsense lady with a great sense of humour and polymathic talents. Speaking in a weird and wonderful mix of German and Cork accents she explained how she fought tooth and nail to turn round this property that she fell in love with and bought before even having it surveyed. It is called Rock Cottage because it was built on a huge rock — which explains the split levels of the ground floor. The results today, as the hard work continues, are a revelation. People tend to book in for one night and end up staying several as Barbara's excellent cooking and enticing bedrooms cast their spell. The bedrooms are in simple bright colours with wood floors and pine beds, sitting areas with wicker chairs and table — and views are over lightly-wooded paddocks, including 21 fruitabix-addicted sheep, a horse and a donkey. A five-minute stroll up the hill and you can see the sea. You are within easy striking distance here of the dramatically beautiful Mizen Head, Ireland's most southwesterly point. Barbara has been successful as shoe designer, knitwear designer, chef. She is also successful at running a friendly B&B with excellent food.

Rooms: 3: 2 family with en suite shower; 1 double sharing bathroom.
Price: £20 — £25 p.p. Sing. supp. £0 — £10.
Breakfast: Included — extensive menu.
Meals: Dinner from £22 (three courses). Lighter meals also on request.
Closed: Never!

How to get there: From Cork take N71. Just before Bantry turn left signed to Durrus. In Durrus take Goleen road left. 8 miles from Durrus past small cemetery, 1st gate on right.

Map Ref No: 15

Shiro

Ahakista
Durrus
Co. Cork

Tel: 027-67030
Fax: 027-67206

Kei and Werner Pilz

Kei is an exuberant and charming Japanese lady and people drive all the way from Dublin for the night to eat at Shiro, the best Japanese restaurant in Ireland. She cooks while husband Werner describes himself as the oldest waiter in the world at 79. Ahakista (which sounds as though it really were in Japan) is one of the last places one would expect to find hidden away near dramatic Sheep's Head, one of the extremities of Ireland. The six or seven main courses all looked mouth-watering on the day I visited. The restaurant consists of only four tables separated where necessary by Japanese screens and there are wonderful views across fine gardens of trees, palms (and peacock) out to sea. Also in the garden is the cottage with sloping ceilings, a downstairs kitchen, sitting room and shower room with a little fireplace and a lovely conservatory. The all-round experience is a great excuse for a couple to splash out. The wherewithal for breakfast is provided but guests must cook it themselves.

Rooms: 1 cottage for two people — shower room downstairs.
Price: £200 — £400 per week for the cottage.
Breakfast: Food included and provided. Cook for yourself in the cottage.
Meals: Dinner £41 set menu. Reservation only. 7-9 p.m.
Closed: December 22nd — Feb 1st.

How to get there: From Cork take N71 to Bandon, Drimoleague to Bantry. Just before Bantry turn left to Durrus. In Durrus turn right to Ahakista. Shiro in middle of village to right (signed).

146

Dromquinna Manor Hotel

Kenmare
Co. Kerry

Tel: 064-41657
Fax: 064-41791
E-mail: dromquinna@tinet.ie
www: www.kenmare.com/dromquinna/

Mike and Sue Robertson

Dromquinna reflects the inexhaustible creative energy of Mike and Sue. The emphasis is on informality, relaxation and the water activities made possible by the hotel's wonderful position on the shore of Kenmare Bay. The large 1850s building is entered through the wood-panelled Great Hall with its sofas, fireplace, atrium and gallery. There is a Chinese-style bar and the large, airy conservatory dining area which looks over the bay has draped mirrors and a green 'grass' carpet which gives breakfast an *al fresco* feel. Lawns lead down past an adventure playground to the jetty and bistro, a focal point for sun-loving water-skiers, canoeists, rowers, sailors, tube-riders and windsurfers — and anyone who enjoys a Sunday afternoon barbecue with jazz music. Add to this a variety of interesting and informal rooms with views (some with four-posters), a wonderful tree house room, three well-publicised ghosts and the friendliest staff to be found in any hotel of comparable size. This is ideal for families, and the hill and water scenery makes it idyllic for walkers.

Rooms: 46: 27 in house, all with en suite bathroom; 1 tree house (sic); 18 new bedrooms in annexe, all with en suite bathrooms.
Price: £25 — 65 p.p. Sing. supp. £20 — depending on season and room.
Breakfast: Included — full Irish.
Meals: Dinner £18.50 set menu, (à la carte too); à la carte Sunday lunch £9.95; Bistro for dinner, lunch and BBQs.
Closed: Never!

How to get there: From Kenmare take Killarney Rd out of town. After 0.5 miles turn left towards Sneem opposite garage. 3 miles later gates with sign on left.

Shelburne Lodge

Cork Rd
Kenmare
Co. Kerry

Tel: 064-41013
Fax: 064-42135

Maura O'Connell-Foley

They say in Kenmare that Maura has the Midas touch. Everything she does she does brilliantly whether it be her wonderful atmospheric restaurants or Shelburne Lodge itself. Lovely yellow bedrooms with huge mirrors, king-size beds, limed antique furniture, rugs on wooden floors; all are proof of a great eye for interior design. This 1740s house is country-style elegant and extremely welcoming. The whole family are easy and friendly and it is a joy to check in, settle on a sofa by a large log fire with the tea that appears by magic and discover from a very knowledgeable Tom what to do round Kenmare. Walks up steep country lanes take you quickly to positions where you have a sweeping view of the Kenmare 'River' and the idyllic surrounding hills. In the evening don't forget to book into Maura's restaurant, 'Packies', which is buzzing and where the food is simple and delicious.

Rooms: 7: 3 king-size doubles; 2 queen-size doubles; 2 twins: all with en suite bath.
Price: £30 — £45 p.p. Sing. supp. £10.
Breakfast: Included — full Irish.
Meals: Packies Restaurant in Kenmare.
Closed: October 31st — Easter.

How to get there: From Killarney take N71 to Kenmare — follow sign to Kilgarvan (Cork Rd). Shelburne Lodge 0.5 miles on the left.

148

Map Ref No: 16

Sallyport House

Glengarriff Road
Kenmare
Co. Kerry

Tel: 064-42066
Fax: 064-42067

Arthur Family

Kenmare is one of my favourite towns in Ireland, the hub for the rings of Kerry and Beara, looking down the Kenmare 'River' for 50 kms past islands to the sea. Sallyport House was built in 1932 and has high standards of comfort. All the bedrooms, which run off a central landing, have full baths and mod cons (I didn't see any trouser presses though!), lots of space and light (sometimes three windows), thick carpets and lovely views over the orchard and the Park Hotel, Muxnaw Mountain, the Caha Mountains and the Kenmare River. There is also a honeymoon four-poster with hearts on the lace surround. Walks from Sallyport take you through to the park or you can stroll along the river in the evening. Breakfast is wonderful, with smoked salmon on the menu. When I visited the staff, even though at the beck and call of visiting foreign bigwigs remained friendly. This is luxury B&B.

Rooms: 5: 1 twin/double, 2 double, 1 family and 1 four-poster: all with en suite bath.
Price: £40 — £45 p.p.
Breakfast: Included — full Irish.
Meals: Available in Kenmare where the food is excellent.
Closed: November 1st — Easter.

How to get there: From Killarney take N71 towards Bantry. Follow Bantry signs thro' Kenmare. Sallyport on left before suspension bridge.

Map Ref No: 16

Ceann Mara

Kenmare
Co. Kerry

Tel: 064-41220
Fax: 064-41220

Thérèse Hayes

It is typical of Thérèse's innate modesty that she didn't put her house forward for consideration because she thought it was too modern. It may be a modern house but few people manage to be as likeable as Thérèse, and few houses have such a magnificent setting. Her garden ("my garden is like a favourite child") extends from the back of the house until it reaches the waters of Kenmare Bay, which is framed in turn by the Caha Mountains behind. This is a bird-watcher's paradise and the sunsets alone can be reason enough to stay here. Thérèse, a geography and English teacher at the local secondary school during term-time, takes great care of her guests, providing memorable breakfasts that feature kedgeree, local cheeses, stewed fruits and home-made scones, as well as the usual Irish fry. Her bedrooms are small and sweet, but no TV. It's part of her philosophy to encourage (not force!) her guests to listen to music or read a book in the very comfortable sitting room instead. One room has the view through purposefully large windows and must be the one to go for. Wonderful value.

Rooms: 4: 1 twin with en suite shower; 1 double with en/s bath; 2 doubles with en suite shower.
Price: £18 p.p. Sing. supp £7.
Breakfast: Included — full Irish.
Meals: Dinner by arrangement: £15 — but great restaurants in Kenmare.
Closed: End September — June 1st.

How to get there: From Kenmare follow signs to Kilgarvan (Cork Rd). 1 mile from Post Office, just past ruined church, house signed to right down 100-yd drive.

150

Map Ref No: 16

Ard Cuan

Ring of Kerry Rd
Tahilla, Sneem
Co. Kerry

Tel: 064-82526

Mary and Tom Ryan

Mary and Tom are extraordinarily friendly and run this neat little B&B from their brand new family house on a hill right on the Kerry Way. There are lots of windows which maximise the house's high position looking out to sea. Bedrooms upstairs are filled with light and have wooden floors, pressure showers, plain white walls and long views over the Caha Mountains. The house is on the family's farm and you can walk out of the back gate here and straight up a mountain blanketed with gorse and heather. Mary is exactly the sort of person you hope will be running your B&B. She loves having people there and will do all in her power to ensure you fully enjoy the area and, more importantly, your stay. So you have it all: people you warm to, in a lovely location, very clean, uncluttered and… a very personal B&B. Eat at the Vestry restaurant, in a church surrounded by a still-used cemetery!

Rooms: 3: 1 family, 1 twin and 1 double: all with en suite shower.
Price: £17 — £20 p.p. Sing. supp. £5.
Breakfast: Included — full Irish.
Meals: Available in Sneem and Kenmare.
Closed: Christmas Week.

How to get there: Take Killarney road out of Kenmare for 0.5 miles. Turn left signed to Sneem and follow Ring of Kerry Rd for 9 miles. House signed on right on a small hill (2 miles after Blackwater Bridge).

Map Ref No: 15

151

Derreensillagh

Castlecove
Co. Kerry

Tel: 064-45347
Fax: 064-45347

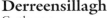

Tim and Bronwen Youard

Everyone must circumnavigate the Ring of Kerry at least once in their lives and Derreensillagh is a gem. I made a complete horlicks of finding the Youards, but normal visitors will have no trouble as it's right on the Ring itself and built up the hill behind. Below the house there is a colony of up to 80 seals to visit; above, the views get more spectacular the higher you climb... and right at the top they have a small plateau garden wilderness, to sit in in summer. From here you walk out into pure countryside. Tim and Bronwen are very entertaining, very caring and they have manipulated this sweet, old, beamed family farmhouse so that it is completely wheelchair-friendly. This means ramps outside and surreptitious design inside! No ugly chrome bars. The whitewashed, self-contained bedrooms are charming with wooden ceilings, seagrass matting floors, hot towel rails and every conceivable little pampering extra your heart could desire. Horsehair mattresses are hand-made; sheets are pure cotton, pillow cases antique and embroidered. There are radios, chocolates, notepaper, hairdryer, tea, coffee, fresh milk, jar of sweeties. You really do get looked after here. They smoke their own salmon which appears at breakfast

Rooms: 2/3: 1 double with en/s bath; 1 two-room family suite sleeping 4/5 en/s shower (adapted for wheelchair).
Price: £25 p.p. Sing. supp. £5.
Breakfast: Included — full Irish / Continental buffet.
Meals: Good food in Sneem and Caherdaniel. Packed lunch £5
Closed: Never!

How to get there: From Kenmare take N70 to Sneem, continue on N70 signed to Waterville. After 6 miles pass 'Community Alert' sign — house on next right-hand bend, 1 mile before Castlecove.

152   Map Ref No: 15

Iskeroon

Bunavalla
Caherdaniel
Co. Kerry

Tel: 066-9475119
Fax: 066-9475488
E-mail: iskeroon@iol.ie
www: http:/homepages.iol.ie/~iskeroon/

Geraldine and David Hare

David and Geraldine are an easy-going young couple who have renovated a wonderfully difficult-to-find, one-storey house right by the sea on the Ring of Kerry. All the rooms are in bold William Morris colours and there is space, light and air. The lay-out is unusual with bedrooms on one side of a corridor and bathrooms and loos on the other. This is a warm house in winter with underfloor heating and peat fires — even in a couple of the bedrooms. But really it must be seen in summer when Iskeroon comes into its own. A little path runs through a restored semi-tropical garden with tree-ferns and winds down to a private jetty where the sea is as clear as a bell. The water is shallow and safe and David also uses the jetty for fishing and lobster-potting. If he has time (normally he's a TV producer) he'll take guests fishing with him. Geraldine uses this remarkably tranquil place as inspiration for her painting. Iskeroon has lovely views, the food is great and there is a lot to do. What else could you want?

Rooms: 3: 2 doubles and 1 twin: all with own bathroom (not en suite, dressing gowns provided).
Price: £35 p.p. Sing. supp. £10.
Breakfast: Included — full Irish.
Meals: Dinner £18. (Please give 24 hours notice.)
Closed: October 31st — May 1st.

How to get there: Between Caherdaniel and Waterville. At Scarriff Inn take road down hill signed Bunavalla Pier all the way to bottom, bearing left at each hairpin. At pier, turn left through gate marked 'private', over beach to very end. House is pink.

Map Ref No: 15

153

The Old Farmhouse

Minard West   **Tel:** 066-9157346
Lispole
Co. Kerry

Jill Sanderson

Two very friendly lurchers will pre-empt their mistress and welcome you enthusiastically to The Old Farmhouse first. Jill has lived here for over nine years after an interesting and varied life both at home and abroad including, finally, running a bookshop on the east coast of England. A keen sailor, she owned and sailed a lovely 11-ton teak sloop for 16 years. Now she has settled for a 130-year-old stone house and three acres, establishing a three-quarter acre hillside garden. Hardy flowering perennials are her speciality nowadays: she grows them out of doors and sells them. This is a television-free house — oh bliss! — and is ideal for the discerning walker and nature lover. The furniture is a mixture of family things and lovingly-restored local pieces such as a traditional Irish dresser. There are books and pictures all over the place and every room has breathtaking views of Dingle Bay. Rooms are simple but inviting, with no discordant note. Sit out at the front on a sunny day enclosed by a low stone wall with a cup of tea and a slice or two of banana bread; or retreat into the sitting room on less clement days and take comfort from the turf fire.

Rooms: In separate wing: 2 twins sharing shower room.
Price: £17 p.p. (2-night stay min). OR: 1 twin en suite available at £45 for 2 sharing (min. stay 2 nights).
Breakfast: Included — full Irish.
Meals: Farmhouse supper £9 (occ).
Closed: Never!

How to get there: From Tralee left at Sullivan's Bar towards Lispole. Take uphill road to Minard castle. At top first right. Continue for 1km. Single-storey pink house with white garden walls and black iron gates on right.

Map Ref No: 15

Greenmount House

Gortonora
Dingle
Co. Kerry

Tel: 066-9151414
Fax: 066-9151974

Mary and John Curran

Although not the most beautiful house in the world from the outside, Greenmount has been cleverly designed on the inside by a young local architect. The result is very large, split-level suite-style bedrooms with simple wallpaper, thick carpets, sitting area and doors that lead out onto a balcony. The standard rooms have the same facilities but are smaller (as you'd expect). Sitting on a hill you have views here over Dingle Bay (somewhere containing its famous resident, Fungi the dolphin)... and, of course, one of the main reasons for coming to Dingle anyway is the fabulous walking plus the dramatic cliff, hill and sea scenery. Mary and John are wonderfully friendly and they really do seem to love the business — Mary must do after 20 years! — and want guests to feel that this is a place to relax and chat. No pretension here. (N.B. The Dingle Peninsula is very busy in mid-summer.)

Rooms: 12: 6 suites all with bathroom; 6 standard rooms all with en suite shower.
Price: £20 — £35 p.p. Sing. supp. £10.
Breakfast: Included — full Irish.
Meals: Available in town.
Closed: December 20th — 27th and one flexible holiday.

How to get there: From Killarney take road for Killorglin; turn right past Killarney golf club signed Milltown/Castlemaine. Follow signs to Dingle. Go into town, right at roundabout, right at next junction, up hill on left.

Map Ref No: 15

155

Gorman's Clifftop Restaurant

Glaise Bheag
Ballydavid, Dingle
Co. Kerry

Tel: 066-9155162
Fax: 066-9155003
E-mail: gormans@tinet.ie

Sile (Sheila) and Vincent Gorman

Here's a rare opportunity to practise your Irish. This side of the valley is a *gael tacht* region, ie people speak Irish as their first language, which always takes me by (pleasant) surprise. And Sile (Sheila) Gorman is just the person to welcome you in on a howling winter evening — so nice, so down-to-earth. Her home/B&B is a warm refuge out here on the cliffs at the end of Ireland. The position is great looking straight across the bay to the Three Sisters islands and away — on fine days this is heaven. Hire a bike for the Slea Head Drive; explore the interior for the many ancient archaeological sites; or just stare open-mouthed at the sea. The rooms are sweet with big comfy beds, stripped-pine cupboards and dressers, all in simple, warm, attractive colours. Sile and Vincent also run a small restaurant in the house — a friendly, wood-furnished place with wonderful food from Vincent's Ballymaloe-inspired repertoire. The Gormans are a naturally hospitable family and you're encouraged to come out into the room with the fire. I liked everything here: people, food, position, rooms — and it's great value too.

Rooms: 3: 2 double/triple with en suite shower; 1 double with en suite shower.
Price: £18.50 p.p. Sing. supp. £3 — £6.50.
Breakfast: Included — full Irish.
Meals: Restaurant fully open March — October: set menus from £12.50. À la carte too. By arrangement out of season.
Closed: 2 days at Christmas. Book out of season.

How to get there: From Dingle out of town with harbour on left to roundabout west of town. Go straight across (NOT left across the bridge) signed An Fheothanach. 8 miles up hill to coast. House on left by the round house.

Map Ref No: 15

Castlemorris House

Ballymullen
Tralee
Co. Kerry

Tel: 066-7180060
Fax: 066-7128007

Mary and Paddy Barry

Castlemorris House, only open one year, is not just a convenient stopping-off post between the Dingle Peninsula and the jewels of County Clare to the north. In fact many people use it as a base from which to head off in all directions. An imposing Georgian house with wooden sash windows (more of a treat in Ireland than it should be!), Castlemorris stands on high ground on the edge of town, so views are over the Slieve Mish mountains in one direction, and over the roofscape of Tralee in the other. The drawing and dining rooms have bay windows, pelmeted curtains, real fires in winter, thick carpets; and then there's a lovely wide staircase that leads up to the bedrooms. Beds are either massive zip'n'links or wrought-iron with draped bedheads. The rooms are large and furnished for simplicity — a sofa may be placed at the end of your bed — and the decoration is equally demure. I liked the proportions of the rooms up in the eaves best. Quality rather than elaboration is the style here. The showers have power. And Mary and Paddy are very friendly hosts.

Rooms: 6: 1 double en/s bath; 3 doubles/twins en/s sh; 1 double en/s sh; 1 d/twin en/s bath; 1 extra bathroom.
Price: £30 p.p. Sing. supp. £10.
Breakfast: Included — full Irish.
Meals: Dinner £20 (3 courses). Wine licence.
Closed: Never!

How to get there: From Limerick take N21 to Tralee; just as you approach town go L at first roundabout signed Dingle. Half a mile to T-junction. Right here, house immediately on right.

Map Ref No: 16

157

Fitzgerald's Farmhouse & Riding Centre

Mount Marian
Abbeyfeale Hill,
Abbeyfeale
Co. Limerick

Tel: 068-31217
Fax: 068-31558

Kathleen Fitzgerald

Your kids are going to love this place. Kathleen and the gentle giant Tim have really found themselves in running their riding centre, animal sanctuary and B&B. Lots of baby goats, kittens, ducks, rabbits, chickens and lambs inhabit a magical, pathed and ponded petland. And there is a touch of the wild west in the pine-poled bunkhouse and campfire singalongs at the children's summer riding camps. You, however, will probably be more comfortable in the pretty, lightly painted rooms with patchwork quilts, sheepskin rugs and separate entrance. Breakfast and dinner are served on blue gingham in a pink-painted, pine-floored dining room. But don't let that keep you from the bustle of kitchen hearth, the indoor ring and stables or even a gallop on the beach with a horse from this busy horse farm. They promote hunting and riding on the premises. Only one rural mile off the N21 this could be just the place for a stopover on your journey to Kerry. Fitzgerald's is a rare, welcoming and affordable place to take your kids.

Rooms: 6: 2 doubles, 3 twins and 1 family: all with en suite bathroom.
Price: £18 p.p. Sing. supp. £6.
Breakfast: Included — full Irish or Continental.
Meals: Dinner £12.
Closed: Never!

How to get there: From Limerick take N21 towards Tralee for 40 miles into Abbeyfeale. Left in square at O'Rourke's Bar. House signed. 1 mile, house on left.

Map Ref No: 16

Ballyteigue House
Rockhill
Bruree
Co. Limerick

Tel: 063-90575
Fax: 063-90575
E-mail: ballyteigue@tinet.ie
www: htpp://homepage.tinet.ie/~ballyteigue

Richard and Margaret Johnson

A lovely Georgian farmhouse and a merry greeting await you at Ballyteigue. It really has everything — beautiful furniture in big beautiful rooms, log fires and a colourfully mature garden, the whole perched high in lush, green Ballyhoura dairy pasture and looking out over the tall, rounded humps of the Galtee Mountains. It's a big family — mostly grown up now — that still gathers in Margaret's busy cheerful kitchen. Do not even suggest that the scones or gooseberry jam might be from other hands. She also has a strong and vivacious sense of colour, sensitively guided by tradition. The bright red front door, smiling in its white Georgian façade, illustrates her taste for contrast. You see this again in walls painted in defining tones with dado and picture rails carefully picked out and the deep reds and browns of old oak and mahogany set off by the light from those tall, wide windows. There is a courtyard at the back and, beyond that, a small farm; Richard, a retired vet, keeps a few horses and some cattle in their field next to the garden. *Please book in advance in the off-season.*

Rooms: 5: 3 doubles and 1 twin en suite. 1 single with separate bathroom.
Price: £20 — £25 p.p. Sing. supp. £5.
Breakfast: Included — full Irish.
Meals: Dinner £18 on request. Packed lunches on request.
Closed: December 15th — February 15th.

How to get there: 7 miles south of Croom, through O'Rourke's Cross, take next right, signposted past Rockhill Church, and take lane to right (signposted) 1 mile from N20.

Map Ref No: 11

The Mustard Seed at Echo Lodge

Ballingarry
Co. Limerick

Tel: 069-68508
Fax: 069-68511

Daniel Mullane

This golden Victorian mansion, perched on the side of the dell with the village below, is a busy monument to indulgence and comfort. Every care has been taken: power showers in the bathrooms, a slopey-ceilinged suite, handmade Connemara carpets and the best beds. With its pine floors, beautiful rich rugs and glowing bright red and yellow halls, the Mustard Seed is bursting with colour and the cheerful vibrancy of Dan Mullane. He is an astonishingly energetic, knowledgeable, perfectionist hospitality genius. Pouring the fresh juices at breakfast, planning the two old ladies' day out in Adare, welcoming the ambassador back from his bike ride, plucking greens from the garden, supervising his renowned restaurant, then pouring the nightcaps, his, and his young staff's, life is a vortex in which you are effortlessly cocooned. Dan takes a month off every year to go backpacking, and gathers, discriminatingly and eclectically, maps, hangings, pictures, Chinese silk prints and new recipes. If your palate becomes jaded with all these delights — and the food is spectacular — there are six easy solutions: each one a local bar.

Rooms: 10: 1 family and 6 doubles; 3 twins: all en suite.
Price: £60 — £75 p.p. Sing. supp. £25.
Breakfast: Included — full Irish.
Meals: Dinner: £30.
Closed: December 24th — 26th and all Feb.

How to get there: From Limerick take N21 through Adare. Left just after village, signed to Ballingarry. Follow signs. Mustard Seed right at village crossroads.

160

Map Ref No: 11

Reens House
Ardagh
Co. Limerick

Tel: 069-64276 mob:086-8177895

Tilly Curtin

Firelight twinkles off the cut glass and deep polished marquetry cabinets. Deep reds and greens rise with a warmth and comfort from carpet and upholstery. Tilly will serve you tea, with a laugh that really does tinkle. It used not to be this way. She remembers this lounge had a mud floor 60 years ago. Her family's Jacobean farmhouse (the oldest in County Limerick) has been fully renovated since, leaving little trace of its antiquity. Her son's young family lives in the rear extension. Larry, a farmer, may even come in at your hearty breakfast to shake hands and explain that morning's bellowing bull (it was penned up close to the cows in season). Tilly is totally house proud — all is spotlessly clean and especially comfortable. No dust gathers on the samovar, hunting prints or buffalo horns and the brass log chest is forever gleaming. So, too, the big arched hall window. It is pleasant to kick back in the conservatory's bamboo loungers and look up the long avenue. That way lies the main road to Kerry and Adare only a few minutes away.

Rooms: 3: 1 family and 1 twin en suite; 1 double with separate bathroom.
Price: £20 p.p. Sing. supp. £7.
Breakfast: Included — full Irish.
Meals: Available locally.
Closed: November 1st — March 31st.

How to get there: From Limerick take N20 for Cork (10 miles). After Patricks Well roundabout take N21 for Tralee. Past Rathkeale 3.5 miles. House signed on right down driveway off N21.

Map Ref No: 11

Sandfield House

Castleroberts
Adare
Co. Limerick

Tel: 061-396119
Fax: 061-396119

Margaret and John Shovlin

Stay in this sturdy, 1970s red-brick house en route to the Dingle Peninsula or Adare sightseeing. Service is comprehensive — Margaret has many American regulars, so there are little boxed shower caps and mini-shampoos in the modern bathrooms and waffles on the varied breakfast menu. The rooms are cool and restful with desks, super comfy beds, big radiators and sheepskin rugs from the Donegal mother-in-law. The mood is set by the darkwood fireplace, hunting prints, muted red and yellow hallways. Margaret and John — head waiter at the renowned Dunraven Arms Hotel for 17 years — know all the options which include the nearby medieval priory, friary and churches, Desmond Castle and stunning Adare Manor and estate. Close too is unsung Limerick, Ireland's third largest city, while the Golden Vale with its rich countryside and woodlands is perfect for gentle walking, fishing and, of course, golfing. Or you may prefer the very private patio and the scent of roses.

Rooms: 4: 1 family, 2 doubles and 1 twin: all en suite.
Price: £19 — £23 p.p.
Breakfast: Included — full Irish.
Meals: Not available.
Closed: 1st November — 1st March.

How to get there: From Limerick and N20 take N21 (Killarney/Tralee Rd) towards Adare. 1 mile before Adare turn left at crenellated gatehouse at beginning of high wall on N21 and continue for 2 miles — house on right.

Map Ref No: 11

Ash Hill Stud

Ash Hill
Kilmallock
Co. Limerick

Tel: 063-98035
Fax: 063-98752

Belinda and Simon Johnson

Ash Hill is typical of many lovely old Irish houses. It was allowed to fall into a degree of dilapidation from which the present encumbents are lovingly rescuing it year by year. It sits at the end of a long drive and forms one side of an impressive stable yard where Simon keeps his horses. This was originally the ancestral pile of Colin ("Gulf War") Powell's family, but today the Johnsons are breathing new life into the old bricks. Rooms are enormous throughout the house and in winter it is a joy to retreat into the snug and hunker down by the roaring fire. There is one downstairs bedroom but I would recommend the others if you can get them — impressive spaces with huge bathrooms. There are eye-catching features throughout the house such as the 18th-century ceilings, the arched window in the children's room (my particular favourite), antique bath tubs, the wood panelling and the plasterwork. Everywhere the house oozes style and potential and Simon and Belinda are mad on it. A friendly laid-back couple who will certainly look after you well. *They also have a lovely self-catering apartment in the converted stable wing.*

Rooms: 4: 1 double with en suite bath; 1 double/triple en/s bath; 1 triple en/s bath; 1 twin sharing bath.
Price: £30 p.p. Sing. supp. £10 depending on season.
Breakfast: Included — full Irish.
Meals: Dinner £20 — £30 depending on number of courses. By arrangement only.
Closed: Christmas and New Year.

How to get there: From Limerick at Tipperary roundabout take south ring road — next roundabout (Kilmallock roundabout) take R512 for 20 miles into Kilmallock. Turn right in centre of town onto R515. 0.5 miles first gates on right.

Map Ref No: 11

Carlow
•
Kilkenny
•
Waterford
•
Wexford
•

The South-East

Sherwood Park House

Ballon
Co. Carlow

Tel: 0503-59117
Fax: 0503-59355

Patrick and Maureen Owens

You drive through the original gate-piers past magnificent great trees and pretty rosebeds to this much-admired example of Georgian style and harmony; it is unusual in Ireland in having four storeys. The reason for tall country houses being so rare may be guessed from one fact: this house has sunk some six feet since it was built in 1730. But the sense of enduring graciousness is solidly entrenched, though there are some interesting sloping floors. Ceilings are high, the staircase is finely elegant, the rooms big with welcoming, well-used armchairs, a thick red carpet in the drawing room, a large polished table and marble fireplace in the dining room where guests eat together. Music is important here — the old flat-top piano in the hall and the grand piano are played regularly — and there are plants everywhere. Paddy and Maureen are happy to greet you and show you up to your room where you will find a half-tester bed and a massive cupboard in the 'master' bedroom, brass or four-poster beds and masses of space in the attic rooms. An enchanting house and lovely owners.

Rooms: 4: 2 suites with en suite bath and shower; 2 doubles/twins with en suite bath and shower.
Price: £25 p.p. Sing. supp. £7.
Breakfast: Included — full Irish.
Meals: Dinner £20.
Closed: Never!

How to get there: N9 south from Naas to Carlow, then N80 towards Wexford, to Ballon. Through Ballon, turn left at 2nd crossroads, signed to house.

Map Ref No: 13

164

Lorum Old Rectory

Kilgreaney
Bagenalstown
Co. Carlow

Tel: 0503-75282
Fax: 0503-75455
E-mail: 100757.16@compuserve.com

Bobbie and Don Smith

What a fine honest face this house has! And what a lovely family you find inside it! Bobbie and Don have three daughters and the piano and flute are clearly not just for decoration. You feel at home as soon as you step inside the front door to be welcomed into the Old Rectory's thick-rugged, marble-fireplaced embrace. Bobbie has won awards for her cooking and you all sit round the big old dining table to feasts of, for example, rack of lamb or fillet of chicken, soup first, sorbet afterwards, a vast Irish cheeseboard if you have room at the end. Many of the ingredients are locally organically grown and the atmosphere is utterly, delightfully Irish (New Zealand Don converted long ago). Up the creaky old stairs, the bedrooms are warm and cosy, Don's Jacob sheep speak pastorally through the windows, there may be views over the Blackstairs Mountains, split-level facilities that respect the original shape of the house, a 16th-century four-poster, a marble fireplace — they are all different and all full of character. A very special place.

Rooms: 5: 4 doubles and 1 double/twin: all with en suite showers.
Price: £30 p.p. Sing. supp. £8.
Breakfast: Included — full Irish.
Meals: Dinner £20.
Closed: December 20th — January 2nd.

How to get there: From Bagenalstown take R705 direction Borris for 4 miles. House signed on left.

Map Ref No: 13

Abbey House

Jerpoint Abbey
Thomastown
Co. Kilkenny

Tel: 056-24166
Fax: 056-24192

Helen Blanchfield

There's been a building standing on the site of Abbey House since the 11th century; this house was built in about 1700. It is sandwiched between the great ruins of Jerpoint Abbey and the mill race of the river Arrigle. Attached to the house is the old mill with a wheel that attracts experts from round the world. Inside, regular-sized bedrooms are homely, and special for their views from both sides of the house. Helen is wonderful with everybody and provides the house with its memorably friendly and relaxed feeling. There are few rules. Breakfast is available until 2 p.m. (try the pan-fried trout from the river). This is a great place from which to roam the wonderful countryside round Thomastown and Inistioge — the River Nore bisects sweeping green valleys here.

Rooms: 6: 4 doubles, 1 twin and 1 single: all with en suite shower or bath.
Price: £18 — £25 p.p. Single occupancy £25 — £30.
Breakfast: Included — full Irish.
Meals: Dinner £17.50. BYO wine.
Closed: December 22nd — 30th.

How to get there: Out of Thomastown on the N9 towards Waterford 1.5 miles opposite Jerpoint Abbey.

Map Ref No: 13

Berryhill

Inistioge
Co. Kilkenny

Tel: 056-58434   mobile: 087-461532
Fax: 056-58434

George and Belinda Dyer

This is an area you will want to visit: a blissful green valley frames the River Nore in a wedge, so clean-cut as it meanders mazily through meadows and under old stone bridges. And there is nowhere better perched for viewing it than Berryhill. The house was built on a hillside in 1780 and set in 250 family-farmed acres so there are wonderful walks all over the property. As the brochure has it, "each field has an even more stunning view than the last". The land even has river frontage for picnics or fishing and there is a mirth-provoking cross-country croquet course on the front lawn. Bedrooms inside, meanwhile, are animal-themed and decorated accordingly: Frog with verandah? Pig or Elephant suite? The suites have their own dressing/sitting area with the latest glossy mags and a collection of novels. Comfort is a priority. The honesty bar for the drinks trolley in the elegant drawing room is typical of George and Belinda's attitude to their guests. Sheep, fan-tails, chickens, all potter about the place, adding to the cosy farmyard atmosphere of this most hospitable refuge.

Rooms: 3 suites, all with bathrooms and dressing rooms/sitting areas.
Price: £40 p.p. Sing. supp. £10.
Breakfast: Included — full Irish.
Meals: For groups of 6 or more only, by arrangement. 6 good restaurants recommended otherwise.
Closed: November 1st — April 20th.

How to get there: From Thomastown take R700 to Inistioge — through village, cross bridge keeping right. Next L (Graiguenamanagh Rd). First R, then 2nd entrance on L at gate lodge.

Map Ref No: 13

Belmore
Jerpoint Church
Thomastown
Co. Kilkenny

Tel: 056-24228
BELMORE@TINET.IE

Rita and Joe Teesdale

This old hunting lodge, built around 1790 for Lord Belmore, is a wonderful place to stay, especially if you're keen on golf or fishing. The River Nore runs through the property, providing two miles of free salmon (licence required) and trout fishing, with more extensive waters available at the local club at very reasonable rates. There are several golf courses in the area, including an 18-hole championship course at Mount Juliet. Joe and Rita run the 120-acre sheep and barley farm, as well as providing excellent breakfasts, warm welcomes, interesting and unusual accommodation (with stunning views), and lots of information about the area. When you've had enough fishing or golf, you can sit in the drawing room's deep bay window and look out over the Nore Valley, a ruined church, the remains of an abandoned medieval town, and rolling green fields dotted with sheep and mature trees. Or go down the stone-flagged steps to the dining room with its amazing vaulted ceiling. Or just enjoy your own room with its pretty windows (more fantastic views), fireplace and vaulted bathroom. No lunch or dinner, but several excellent restaurants within five miles.

Rooms: 3: 1 twin and 2 doubles: all with en suite showers.
Price: £20 p.p.
Breakfast: Included — full Irish.
Meals: Six excellent restaurants within 5 miles.
Closed: Never!

How to get there: From Kilkenny take R700 to Thomastown. Cross bridge onto N9 (Waterford Rd), turn right after Jerpoint Abbey. House signed to right.

Map Ref No: 13

Cullintra House

The Rower
Inistioge
Co. Kilkenny

Tel: 051-423614
cullhse@indigo.ie
www: http://indigo.ie/~cullhse/

Patricia Cantlon

Cullintra is one of Ireland's most special places. Two guests I met lounging by a log fire waxed lyrical: fantastic food, convivial atmosphere, beautiful rooms and a sense of real effort. Be prepared to let Patricia's eccentricity and whimsy lead you through the experience, which is unforgettable. Cullintra suits those who enjoy something a bit different and my advice is to stay two nights, be prepared to eat your fabulous dinner late (I mean 9.30 p.m. late!); full breakfasts will not start until at least 9.30 a.m. Continental breakfasts are available for those who want to leave early and, if you *are* in a hurry, I suggest you tell Patricia the night before. The rooms she has created are astonishing. From the conservatory-studio to the gallery rooms converted out of old barns, this is Accommodation Art. Come for the whole experience — there's no going into town for supper but who would want to? Patricia loves cats (she has seven) and won't stand for blood sports — foxes come to the garden to feed. The house stands at the foot of Mount Brandon in 230 acres and the views and woodland walks are stunning. Come with an open mind.

Rooms: 6: Can all be doubles, twins, triples as required. Ask when booking for the arrangement you need.
Price: £20 — £25 p.p. Sing. supp. £10.
Breakfast: Included — full Irish.
Meals: Dinner £16. BYO wine. All guests must book for dinner too.
Closed: Never!

How to get there: Cullintra House is 50 minutes from Rosslane Ferryport and 2 hours from Dublin Airport. 6 miles from New Ross on Kilkenny road (R700), 19 miles from Kilkenny. Follow signs.

169   Map Ref No: 18

Knocktopher Hall

Knocktopher
Co. Kilkenny

Tel: 056-68626
Fax: 056-68626
E-mail: jcknock@indigo.ie
www: http://indigo.ie/~jckock/

John and Carmel Wilson

John and Carmel have worked incredibly hard on improving their lovely listed Georgian country house (1740). John's comment to me when I visited was, "If we are going to do something, we like to do it well". The house sits on high ground and overlooks Mount Leinster and the Blackstairs Mountains, surrounded by ten acres of garden and fields. From the top of the house — at least four floors — the views are long and the feeling high. The grounds below are patrolled by a pair of restless peacocks called Sweetpea and Oscar (Wilde). John and Carmel encourage guests to wind down, providing delicious and exotic meals, all home-made (including fabulous pâtés). As for the rooms, downstairs is all high ceilings, floor-to-ceiling windows, antique furniture and curtains, and the huge wood-panelled drawing room is lovely. Bedrooms are special for their antique French beds, their views... and their size. The largest room in the house is probably the largest room in this book — 30 x 20 x 15! John and Carmel are renowned for their hospitality and everything here is served up with great style.

Rooms: 4: 3 doubles and 1 family: 3 with en suite shower, 1 with bath.
Price: £35 p.p. Sing. supp. £10.
Breakfast: Included — full Irish.
Meals: Dinner £25. Wine licence.
Closed: December 15th — January 2nd.

How to get there: From Kilkenny take the N10 south towards Waterford for 11 miles. Pass through Stoneyford. 3 miles on and 0.25 miles before Knocktopher village, turn right (signposted Knocktopher Hall).

Map Ref No: 12

Tuckmill
Danesfort Rd   **Tel: 056-27620**
Bennettsbridge
Co. Kilkenny

Maureen Kennedy

Maureen is irrepressible, a character bubbling over with chat, greatly concerned for her guests' welfare. Des, meanwhile, is more demure in his approach, but equally friendly. They have a modern house in a lovely area of Ireland, half a mile from the gorgeous River Nore valley and only a couple of miles out of Kilkenny town. Culture and countryside on your doorstep and Maureen says they will drop people into Kilkenny for dinner if they want to leave their car and get a taxi back. The rooms at Tuckmill are simple in design, not frilly, with most emphasis being placed on comfort, space, cleanliness, beds... that sort of thing. I, for one, slept like a log when I stayed. The good-sized showers have power, the bath is big and generally the Kennedys have not spared expense in ensuring they only get satisfied customers. Downstairs the sitting room has a cosy coal fire and thick carpets. Breakfast is next to the kitchen, a bustly, chatty affair, and the fry is delicious. Maureen and Des offer very good value in a friendly home.

Rooms: 3: 1 double with en suite shower; 1 double plus single with en suite shower; 1 twin en/s bath and shower.
Price: £15 — £18 p.p. Sing. supp. £5.
Breakfast: Included — full Irish.
Meals: Excellent restaurants in Kilkenny.
Closed: Never!

How to get there: From Kilkenny take road signed Thomastown/New Ross. After 5 miles enter Bennettsbridge, turn right before the bridge, then immediately right again up hill — house 400 metres on left.

Map Ref No: 12

Danville House

New Ross Rd
Kilkenny
Co. Kilkenny

Tel: 056-21512
Fax: 056-21512

Kitty Stallard

This is a real old farmhouse on the outskirts of historic Kilkenny, but you'd never know. The house is 1765 Georgian, surrounded by ancient trees, including oaks from the 1760s, and a lovely walled garden festooned with shrubs and climbers. When I visited there was a heavenly peace in the air with the sun shining and the birds chirruping in the apple orchard. Cromwellian armour and a grandfather clock greet you through the arch of the front door and a very pretty staircase leads up to a big landing and a conversation seat. The four bedrooms are immaculate in pale colours, floral covers (nice not garish), firm beds, timber windows overlooking the paddock. The largest room has a half-tester, windows on both sides and lots of space. Kitty is adamant that the house keep its country feel. Stallards have been here since 1905 farming the 100 acres of dairy cattle to south and west. To north and east you are in Kilkenny itself. Danville is the perfect place from which to see the region — friendly, unpretentious, high standards, great breakfast, rural bliss with old-style charm.

Rooms: 4: 2 triple/twin, 1 twin and 1 double: all with en suite shower.
Price: £18 p.p. Sing. supp. £6.50.
Breakfast: Included — full Irish.
Meals: Available in Kilkenny.
Closed: November 1st — April 1st.

How to get there: From Kilkenny take R700 towards New Ross. House 1 mile on right from the castle.

Butler House

Patrick Street
Kilkenny
Co. Kilkenny

Tel: 056-65707/22828
Fax: 056-65626

Anthony Foley

The front of Butler house gives little away. Right in the middle of Kilkenny, it looks like any large townhouse. In fact it is the dower house to Kilkenny Castle and guests are treated 'out the back' to a large garden and intimate views over the castle itself. As for the house (staff are at pains not to describe it as a hotel), here you will find something very special. Rather than attempting to restore the late 18th-century glory the management turned the refurbishment over to Kilkenny Design. The result: very stylish, very stylised, very 70s. Huge rooms with towering ceilings are sparsely furnished in black wood, uncluttered cream and white walls and carpets, modern paintings, charcoal drawings and carpeted window seats running wall-to-wall. There are rooms with wide bays which look over the castle, and the 'executive suite' has housed the Irish PM a couple of times. Anthony Foley is enthusiastic about his realm and humorous and easy with it. There isn't a place like it in Ireland. Luxury with the personal touch; a townhouse with a view.

Rooms: 14: 1 suite; 3 'superior' rooms; 6 'standard' doubles/twins; 4 singles: all en suite.
Price: £34.50 — £45.50 p.p. Sing. supp. £15.
Breakfast: Included — full Irish.
Meals: Lunch available in the restaurant £6.50 — £10. Open to the public.
Closed: December 24th — 30th.

How to get there: In Kilkenny follow signs for city centre. At 4-street junction (in centre), take signs to Waterford (this is Patrick St). Hotel on left. Park past house on left.

Map Ref No: 12

Blanchville House
Dunbell   **Tel:** 056-27197
Maddoxtown
Co. Kilkenny

Monica and Tim Phelan

Monica would cringe if I said she was the perfect hostess. Nevertheless she is so sympathetic that the very idea that guests might feel in any way neglected would be painful for her. Her large Georgian farmhouse is relaxed and friendly, her food is top-notch, half-tester beds sit on thick carpets by modern bathrooms in large rooms... and views are immeasurable over to Carlow and Kilkenny. Downstairs, original mirrors and gold pelmets, lovely early 19th-century wallpaper and the portrait of Sir James Kearney, who built the house, look down from a height onto one of the mightiest dining tables in Ireland. And, outside, the ruined clocktower stands clockless, an eccentric vestige of the house's originator. This is deep peace; enjoy it. *Self-catering houses now available in converted coach-house.*

Rooms: 6: 4 doubles and 2 twins: all with en suite bath or shower.
Price: £30 — £35 p.p.
Breakfast: Included — full Irish.
Meals: Dinner £20 but must know by noon same day.
Closed: November 1st — March 1st.

How to get there: From Kilkenny take N10 towards Carlow/Dublin. 2 miles out pass Pike Inn. Another half mile turn right signed to Blanchville House. Follow signs and turn left at Connolly's pub. 1st large house on left. Ruined clocktower to right on drive.

Map Ref No: 12   **174**

Swift's Heath

Jenkinstown
Co. Kilkenny

Tel: 056-67653
Fax: 056-67653

Brigitte Lennon

Swift's Heath, one of Ireland's Historic Houses, was built by Godwin Swift in 1651 and was home to his famous nephew Jonathan (1667-1745). It remained in the Swift family until 1970 when the Lennons took it over. Many famous international figures — royalty, writers and artists — have stayed here over the years, and its special cosmopolitan style of grand hospitality is maintained by the present owners. Brigitte is German (an interior designer), with friends from all over the world, and is interested in practically everything, from language to architecture and the amazing history of the house. She's put a refreshingly clean, uncluttered stamp on the massive bedrooms and bathrooms, showing off the ornate architectural features to perfection. Downstairs in the dining room the parquet floor creaks where diners have rocked back on their heels in front of the magnificent marble fireplace for 350 years. For the more active there's a grass tennis court. Approached by a sweeping drive, the house stands in 200 acres of park and farmland, with cedar of Lebanon and weeping beech trees. *Children over 12.*

Rooms: 3: 1 double with en suite shower; 1 twin with en suite shower; 1 twin with private bath.
Price: £30 p.p. No sing. supp.
Breakfast: Included — full Irish.
Meals: Dinner £18.
Closed: December 20th — February 1st.

How to get there: From Kilkenny take N77 for 3 miles. Turn left following N77 signed to Swift's Heath — big gates 3 miles on right.

175

Kilrush House

Freshford
Co. Kilkenny

Tel: 056-32236
Fax: 056-32588

Richard and Sally St George

The St Georges long ago moved out of the castle that lies ruined to one side of this imposing early nineteenth-century house; two hundred years later Richard and Sally find themselves custodians of the family heirlooms. A lot of work has been done to bring the house into the twentieth century and today modern comfort sits comfortably with the antique: the dining room has not changed since 1830, retaining its original wallpaper and the Irish furniture which was designed for the house (1810). Bedrooms are grand, with long views out over fields. Bathrooms have free-standing old-fashioned baths. As well as having a natural, easy-going ability with people, Richard breeds horses and is an expert on Irish history and architecture (you can see why) and Sally is an expert in the kitchen — a perfect combination when opening one's house to overseas visitors. There are 250 acres to roam in along with the sheep and cattle; you can play tennis or croquet or walk out to see the thoroughbred mares and foals. This is a piece of history to enjoy in comfort.

Rooms: 3: All double with en suite bath or shower.
Price: £45 p.p.
Breakfast: Included — full Irish.
Meals: Dinner £15 — £25 p.p. An interesting wine list is extra.
Closed: October 1st — end March.

How to get there: On main Dublin — Cork road (N8) turn left in Johnstown towards Freshford and Kilkenny. Kilrush 10 kms further on right.

Map Ref No: 12

176

Buggy's Glencairn Inn
Glencairn
Co. Waterford

Tel: 058-56232
Fax: 058-56232

Ken and Cathleen Buggy

Ken and Cathleen steadfastly refuse to sound their own trumpet, so I must do it for them. Buggy's has 'a wealth of uniqueness' as one fan put it. Another told me he would be angry if he'd bought our book and not been told about the place — this all before I got there! Buggy's Glencairn Inn is a small pub, a small restaurant and a small B&B — small but perfectly formed. Dump your stuff on your wonderful double bed, have a hot bath, slip downstairs for a pint of Guinness by the log fire in a snug, wooden pub; you will be called through to the even snugger restaurant, where no stone is left unturned in the effort to cater for your needs. Food is utterly delicious. After coffee, return to the pub for a few nightcaps and, if possible, grab Ken and get him to remind you that the world is not such a serious place after all. The man has a gift. If you were driving through the dark wondering where the hell to pass the night and you stumbled upon Buggy's, you would know, at least, that some of your sins were forgiven!

Rooms: 4: 3 doubles and 1 twin: all with en suite bathrooms.
Price: £32 p.p. Sing. supp. £10.
Breakfast: Included — full Irish.
Meals: Dinner about £18.
Closed: Christmas Day, Good Friday, 1st 3 wks in Nov, last wk in Feb, 1st wk in March.

How to get there: Drive out of Lismore for about 0.75 miles on the N72 towards Tallow. Turn R at car showroom. Following signs to Glencairn turn right at Horneybrooks car dealers and Buggy's is 2 miles on the right in Glencairn, by a crossroads.

177

Map Ref No: 17

Hanora's Cottage
Nire Valley
Ballymacarbry
Co. Waterford

Tel: 052-36134
Fax: 052-36540

Seamus and Mary Wall

Nothing could provide a better start to a day out in the mountains than Mary Wall's breakfast — warm nut bread, special-recipe porridge, scones, cheeses, smoked salmon, cream, apricots, plums, cereals... the list is endless, and that's before the scrambled eggs, sweet bacon and coffee. Then after the exertions of the day (your hosts will pack a lunch, if you think you'll need one!) return to Ballymaloe-trained son Eoin's culinary delights, washed down with a good wine. All mod cons are provided in the bedrooms, and just in case the exercise and fine food aren't enough to induce blissful slumber, there is the gentle sound of a nearby stream. Near the Nire River in the forested foothills of the Comeragh Mountains, Hanora's Cottage has an idyllic setting with lovely views from the inside, and the patio to enjoy them from in summer. The lawn rolls down to a pond and a gate leading to the bubbling stream with grassy bank, rhododendrons and an old stone bridge. Trekking on horseback can be arranged and Seamus has expert knowledge of the many local golf courses. *Adults only.*

Rooms: 8: all doubles/twins with en suite bath.
Price: £30 — £35 p.p. Sing. supp. £10.
Breakfast: Included — full Irish.
Meals: Dinner £20.
Closed: December 15th — 27th.

How to get there: From Clonmel cross the bridge from the N24, follow signs to Dungarvan as far as Ballymacarbry. Hanora's signed left over small bridge by Melody's Lounge. 3.5 miles on by the Nire church.

The Old Rectory

Stradbally
Kilmacthomas
Co. Waterford

Tel: 051-293280

Julian and Alison Burkitt

The Burkitts are a warm and intelligent couple who are almost embarrassingly attentive to your comfort and well-being. They like company and are enjoyable conversationalists. The rectory, built round a small courtyard and standing in five acres of its own garden and field, is furnished with great taste. One is ensconced in an enveloping armchair beside log fire, gin and tonic in hand with cat asleep on knee and three dogs asleep at feet, it really is very hard to get up again. Upstairs, the bedrooms have been left as designed, so guests use bathrooms that were built as rooms (rather than yet more cramped showers and ventilator-fans for the 'en suite' cachet!). Old-fashioned carpets, rugs, curtains and furniture — a very high double bed, old school trunks and chests — are set off with flair by the bold blues, pinks and yellows of the painted walls. The comfort of the bedrooms weakens one's resolve to emerge for breakfast. But the seductive smells wafting from the kitchen do the trick. Stradbally is a lovely coastal village with a great cove for summer bathing; drives to the Comeragh mountains and along the coast to Annestown are highly recommended.

Rooms: 4: 3 doubles and 1 small single: all with adjacent bathrooms.
Price: £28 p.p. Sing. supp. £7.
Breakfast: Included — full Irish.
Meals: Dinner £20 by arrangement but The Tannery in Dungarvan is excellent. Light suppers on request: £12.
Closed: Christmas.

How to get there: N25 Cork-Waterford road, turn off at Griffins garage towards Stradbally — 5 miles. Rectory in the centre of the village.

Map Ref No: 18

Annestown House

Annestown
Co. Waterford

Tel: 051-396160
Fax: 051-396474
E-mail: annestownhouse@tinet.ie
www: http://homepage.tinet.ie/~annestown

John and Pippa Galloway

In this location a shack would be enough. It is an added bonus to find on the cliffs at Annestown a lovely 1830s country house, gazing out across the sea on one side and the hills and fields that stretch away to the Comeragh Mountains on the other. Two manicured lawns on different levels entice you to go and peer over the edge; little grassy paths lead down to the cove. All the rooms are large, with lovely views and some have huge beds and modern bathrooms. Downstairs, everything retains its old-fashioned feel. The house is John's family seat and previous Galloways and Pallisers have left their belongings. A billiards room-cum-library has a full-size table and complete sets of 1820s editions of Voltaire and Scott. The Galloways love good company and John remembers fondly those evenings where the piano is played, or a few flakes of snow are excuse enough for an entire house party to stay another night or two. You will love this place, whether playing grass court tennis high above the bay in summer, or huddling round the snug fires in winter after invigorating walks.

Rooms: 5: 1 double with shower en suite; 4 double with bath en suite.
Price: £30 — £32.50 p.p.
Breakfast: Included — full Irish.
Meals: Dinner at £18 — £20; house wines £15.
Closed: December — February except for house parties etc.

How to get there: From Waterford follow signs to Tramore. Through town centre, up steep hill. Continue until sharp bend signed to Annestown (past golf club). Continue into Annestown, house on left (signed).

Map Ref No: 18

The Old Rectory Kilmeaden House

Kilmeaden
Co. Waterford

Tel: 051-384254
Fax: 051-384884

Jerry and Patricia Cronin

On a fine day such as the one on which I happened to visit, Kilmeaden is a rural idyll. Go through the gates and up the drive and crunch to a halt on gravel before the imposing, creeper-clad house. On this hot day doors were open at both ends of the large hall and wrought-iron chairs laid out by the lawn at the back. Here you find a magnificent flower garden, walled in on one side with terraces of vegetables and beds of wonderful roses. The combination of bees, petals, manicured grass lawns, sun and shade made me want to lie down on the grass and go to sleep. Beyond this lovely garden there are paddocks and trees. Local surgeon Jerry and his wife Patricia have done a lot of work on this 200-year-old rectory, opening up the long hall with an arched recess, which now houses the grand piano, and doing up all the rooms; the results are irreproachable. Large bedrooms overlooking the garden are immaculate with thick carpets, excellent new beds, pretty, wooden windows, big white bathrooms with baskets of soaps — one even has a banistered step. Kilmeaden is deeply peaceful. *Children over 12 welcome.*

Rooms: 5: 3 doubles and 2 twins all with en suite bath.
Price: £50 — £60 p.p. Sing. supp. £20.
Breakfast: Included — full Irish.
Meals: Light meals available in the evening. 24 hours notice please.
Closed: October 1st- May 1st.

How to get there: From Waterford take N25 towards Cork for 8 miles. Turn right signed to Carrick-on-Suir. House 300m through gates on right.

Map Ref No: 18

Sion Hill House and Gardens

Ferrybank
Waterford
Co. Waterford

Tel: 051-851558
Fax: 051-851678
E-mail: sionhill@tinet.ie

George and Antoinette Kavanagh

George and Antoinette are a gentle, modest couple who share a passion for their home. George has immersed himself in the house's 200 years of history and paints imaginary word pictures of old Waterford. He will show you the 11th-century Coptic monk that he found carved into the old garden wall (what were Egyptians doing in the area?). Sion Hill House stands high on the hill opposite Waterford and presides over the waterfront and its multi-coloured buildings. Two pavilions sit like guard dogs to the left and right of the house. Bedrooms are well furnished and of a good size; large beds too, and fine views, especially when you consider this is a city address. Plans are afoot to turn the grounds into an exact replica of how they were in 1870; George loves his trees. It's a (nice) surprise to be surrounded by so much green (four acres) and to have so much peace in a large city. They have, to top it all, just won a highly-thought-of environmental award for 'best hotel or guesthouse frontage'.

Rooms: 4: 1 double with en suite shower; 1 family with en suite bath; 1 family with en suite shower; 1 triple with en suite bath.
Price: £21 — £30 p.p. Sing. supp. £6.50 — £10.
Breakfast: Included — full Irish.
Meals: Available locally.
Closed: Christmas.

How to get there: Take N25 over bridge out of Waterford towards Rosslare — the limestone entrance (100m beyond Jury's Hotel sign) with ornate iron gates is on your left.

Map Ref No: 18

Brown's Townhouse

29 South Parade
Waterford
Co. Waterford

Tel: 051-870594
Fax: 051-871923
E-mail: info@brownstownhouse.com
www: http://www.brownstownhouse.com

Leslie and Barbara Brown

Leslie's telephone voice can sound slightly flat but this is greatly misleading as he is friendly and mischievously humorous. The B&B is really his domain while by day Barbara is out accounting for a local firm. They have put a great deal of thought into this Victorian townhouse and the results are charming. They are always enlarging the collection of modern Irish paintings on the walls and bedroom windows are refreshed and jollified by flowered boxes. Sash windows look onto a quiet residential street (easy and safe for parking), at the end of which lies the People's Park. Waterford is not a huge town but it is nice to be so near the lively centre with its buzzing restaurants, cafés and bars — it's no more than a five-minute walk to the waterfront or the Wine Vault restaurant. Bedrooms are very comfortable with big windows, large beds and excellent showers. At the top of the house, reached via a tiny staircase, is a fun orange and blue family room. The other rooms are older in style. Leslie's breakfast includes pancakes and home-made jams and bread, fruit salad and the full fry. Brown's Townhouse is great value.

Rooms: 6: 1 family en/s shower; 1 twin en/s bath; 3 doubles en/s shower; 1 suite with bath and sitting room.
Price: £25 — £30 p.p. Sing. supp. £5.
Breakfast: Included — full Irish and vegetarian.
Meals: Available in Waterford.
Closed: December 20th — December 28th.

How to get there: Arriving in Waterford from Dublin, cross bridge, turn L down the quay, follow road round to R. At 2nd traffic lights after Tower Hotel turn L, over hump-backed bridge, past park. South Parade straight on.

Foxmount Farm

Passage East Rd,
off Dunmore East Rd
Waterford
Co. Waterford

Tel: 051-874308
Fax: 051-854906
E-mail: foxmount@iol.ie
www: URLhttp://www.iol.ie/tipp/foxmount.htm

Margaret and David Kent

David and Margaret Kent have built an awesome reputation over the 30 years she's been looking after her guests at Foxmount. People come back again and again to this peaceful 17th-century farmhouse, secluded in its 200 acres of dairy and beef farm, just three miles from the sea. Margaret is utterly nice, no falseness there — it is clear she is genuinely proud of what she does. And no description would be true to the overall picture without an emphasis on the quality of the food she produces. "I will not deviate from my butter-and-cream policy," she says adamantly. She cooks "naturally", ie her own beef, lamb, wild salmon, fruit (not sprayed), vegetables, free-range eggs and chicken, fresh herbs. Dinners are taken at separate tables, although a dinner-party atmosphere is quite common, and then guests come together for coffee in front of the marble fireplace in the big drawing room. Bedrooms are lovely, with split levels and proper bathrooms. Creeper-framed windows overlook a valley on one side, the farmyard on the other. I'd be happy in any of the rooms.

Rooms: 5: 4 doubles/twins with en suite bath; 1 double and twin with own shower and toilet.
Price: £25 p.p. Sing. supp. £5.
Breakfast: Included — full Irish.
Meals: Dinner £20. Please bring own wine.
Closed: November 1st — March 1st.
How to get there: From Waterford take Dunmore Rd for 3 miles, turn left towards Passage East, follow signs to Foxmount.

Map Ref No: 18

184

Kilmokea Country Manor and Gardens

Great Island
Campile
Co. Wexford

Tel: 051-388109
Fax: 051-388776
E-mail: kilmokea@indigo.ie
www: www.kilmokea.com

Mark and Emma Hewlett

The four rooms at Kilmokea are few and precious. It's one of those rare places where it's hard to find a chink in the armour. Mark and Emma couldn't be nicer (as the manner of the people working for them amply proves) and they have transmogrified Kilmokea so that their few guests are favoured indeed. Wonderful food from the formal walled garden is enjoyed at one table in "dinner-party mode" as the brochure has it. Every room in the house has been made over with flair, taste and even humour. Colours throughout are mellow and warm, carpets are thick, showers are state-of-the-art, bath towels are big and new, beds are wonderful. You will not be disappointed. The house itself is Georgian, positioned on the Barrow estuary on Great Island and surrounded by gardens that cover some seven acres: from the walled garden "a heavy wooden door leads you into the magical world of the woodland garden, a delight to both the keen amateur and the more serious horticulturist". There's a lovely Georgian conservatory for cream teas too.

Rooms: 4: 1 twin with private shower; 2 doubles with en suite bath; 1 four-poster en/s shower.
Price: £38 — £65 p.p.
Breakfast: Included — full Irish.
Meals: Dinner £20.
Closed: Never!

How to get there: From Passage East R733 north past Dunbrody Abbey. After 1.5 miles road swings sharp right — straight on signed Great Island. At T-junction turn left. 2 km to house. From New Ross R733 for Campile — before village look for Kilmokea signs.

Map Ref No: 18

Glendine Country House

Arthurstown
Co. Wexford

Tel: 051-389258
Fax: 051-389258

Tom and Annie Crosbie

Glendine sits up on a hill overlooking the sweep of the Barrow Estuary to the hills on the other side; it is a great place to stop before crossing over to Waterford on the charming car ferry. The house was built in 1830 and Tom and Annie have put a huge amount of effort into its refurbishment, keeping the house's old style. But now all the rooms are comfortable, warm and homely... and everything runs as a family house should. They have three young boys, always on the look-out for new friends, and there are dogs, ponies, sheep and beef cattle. This is a lively household run by a relaxed and friendly couple and you will be thoroughly looked after. There is a self-catering (house-sized) section attached to the house which sleeps six and is very good value at £300 a week. I don't know if apple pie is Annie's speciality, but it is delicious!

Rooms: 4: 1 family with en suite shower; 1 double with bath; 2 doubles/twins with shower.
Price: £20 — £25 p.p. Sing. supp. £7.50.
Breakfast: Included — full Irish.
Meals: Lunch snacks from £1.50, for a sandwich for example.
Closed: Christmas.

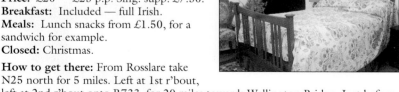

How to get there: From Rosslare take N25 north for 5 miles. Left at 1st r'bout, left at 2nd r'bout onto R733, for 20 miles towards Wellington Bridge. Just before Arthurstown as you go down a hill; gates on right.

Map Ref No: 18

Salville House

Enniscorthy
Co. Wexford

Tel: 054-35252
Fax: 054-35252

Gordon and Jane Parker

Jane receives guests while Gordon works his wizardry in the kitchen. The house sits on the top of a hill, the better to take in the River Slaney and the sunsets. There is a comfortable and cosy sitting room, a log fire for winter and deep armchairs; bedrooms are homely, one pink, one blue, one with yellow stripey wallpaper, and beds have good mattresses and linen. This is an old house extended from the 17th century to the late 19th, with a garden, terrace and serviceable tennis court. The croquet hoops are there for summer. Guests eat together, and extremely well, with veg, fruit and eggs grown or laid at Salville and all other products coming from local organic producers (the results are featured in the Irish Food Guide). Your hosts specialise in 'long weekends with leisurely breakfasts and candlelit dinners. The emphasis is on relaxation.' I can vouch for that. There is also a self-catering annexe.

Rooms: 3: all double: 1 with en suite shower; 1 with en suite bath and shower; 1 with own bath (not en/s).
Price: £22.50 — £25 p.p. Sing. supp. £5.
Breakfast: Included — full Irish.
Meals: Dinner £20 (normally BYO wine).
Closed: Never!

How to get there: N11 just outside Enniscorthy towards Wexford, past sign to Hospital on left. Take next left signed to Salville. Top of the hill keep left. House 0.25 miles on left.

Map Ref No: 19

Ballinkeele House

Ballymurn
Enniscorthy
Co. Wexford

Tel: 053-38105
Fax: 053-38468
E-mail: balinkeel@indigo.ie

Margaret and John Maher

First impressions of Ballinkeele are of space — space, height and light. All the rooms are massive and adorned with a varied and impressive range of Margaret's paintings mixed in with old family pictures. Your reception, in the columned portico, by the three rumbustiously friendly dogs sets the tone. This grand 19th-century house was built by John's great-grandfather and everywhere there is a sense of easy-going, lived-in grandeur. Bedrooms are named by colour and are exquisite. Some have two windows on different walls overlooking the park; one an extended balcony. The jewel in the crown, though, is the master bedroom with its superb four-poster. Outside, John copes with the beef and barley on the surrounding farm. Inside, Margaret presides over mouth-watering meals. The result is a meeting of the elegant and the down-to-earth. A splendid place to relax and go for long walks around the ponds and lakes in the 360 acres of grounds. It genuinely matters to this couple that you are completely at your ease.

Rooms: 5: 3 doubles with en suite shower; 1 twin with en suite bath; 1 twin/double with en suite shower and bath.
Price: £40 — £45 p.p. Blue bedroom and Master bedroom. Others £35. Sing. supp. £10.
Breakfast: Included — full Irish.
Meals: Dinner £25. Wine à la carte. Book before noon on day of arrival.
Closed: November 6th — March 1st.

How to get there: Take N11 going north or south to Oilgate. Turn at lights in centre of village and follow signs to Ballinkeele for 4 miles. Turn left in Ballymurn; first black gates on left.

Map Ref No: 19

188

Churchtown House

Tagoat
Rosslare
Co. Wexford

Tel: 053-32555
Fax: 053-32555

Austin and Patricia Cody

Churchtown House is immaculate. Large elegant rooms, good Irish paintings, bright colours — this house looks (and is!) warm even in the depths of a howling winter Wexford day. All the bedrooms are big and of different shapes, some with bay windows, some with views over the surrounding pastureland, some catering for wheelchair users... and sunlight seems to filter from everywhere, including the atrium well. Despite the pristine state of all the furnishings this remains an easy-going place to stay. This is down to Patricia and Austin who take such pains to ensure guests feel they are in a family home despite the size of the establishment. It is not a hotel, and it doesn't feel like one. Guests — and dogs! — roam freely. Very good value. Stop here for a couple of days to walk the unspoilt beaches before continuing your journey from the Rosslare ferry. *They can garage bikes, trailers, boats on wheels... you name it, they can accommodate it!*

Rooms: 12: 2 family with shower en suite; 5 twins and 5 doubles (half with shower, half with bath en suite).
Price: £25 — £35 p.p. Sing. supp. £10.
Breakfast: Included — full Irish.
Meals: Dinner £19.50 including pre-prandial sherry. Packed lunches (for bird-watchers) on request.
Closed: Mid-November — March. Wintering bird watchers on request.

How to get there: Take N25 2.5 miles from Rosslare Harbour ferry. At Tagoat village, turn right onto R736; house 0.5 miles on left.

Map Ref No: 19

Furziestown House

Tacumshane   **Tel:** 053-31376
Co. Wexford

Yvonne Pim

Unravel a ball of string on your way to Furziestown — it may be difficult to get
away! The coastal lanes of south Wexford are labyrinthine and generally unmarked.
It is the ease with which you are ushered into Yvonne's small 'womb-like' farmhouse
that makes you reluctant to leave. Upstairs the snug low-ceilinged bedroom feels as
if it once belonged to a child — very cosy and bright. The house lies between two
bird-laden lakes and is right on the coast for great walks. But it is Yvonne who really
makes the place special. Notwithstanding all the trouble she takes to make sure
guests eat the freshest home-grown fruit and veg, it is her rare and almost serene
talent of making you feel at home that makes the drive down all those muddy lanes
well worth the effort. A newly-refurbished old stone cowshed in the yard can take
overflow B&B guests or can be rented weekly for self-catering. Although it may
seem that Furziestown is at the back end of nowhere, it's actually not far from the
ferry at Rosslare — handy for the beginning or end of a holiday.

Rooms: 2: 1 double and single with en
suite shower; 1 twin with en suite bath.
Price: £20 p.p.
Breakfast: Included — full Irish.
Meals: Dinner available locally.
Closed: November 1st — After Easter.

How to get there: Ask Yvonne to send
you her excellent little map. In the space
available here I would only make matters
worse!

Map Ref No: 19   **190**

Course, workshops, lessons and facilities available.

A glossary of Irish place names

Ard	High
Ath	Crossing place (ford)
Bally	Townland of (or town)
Cahir or Caher	Ringfort or fortified dwelling
Carrig	Rock
Carrow	Division of land
Clogh	Stone
Clon or Cloon	Field or meadow
Crag	Stony field
Derry or Dar	Oak wood
Don or Doon	Fortified house or ringfort
Drum	Hill
Glen	Valley
Gort	Garden or field
Inis	Island
Kyle	Wood
Kil or Kill	Church
Knock	Hill
Lis or Lios	Ringfort or fortified dwelling
Lough	Lake
Mór/beag	Big/small
Park	Field
Poul	Hole
Rath	Ringfort (earthen ringfort)
Shan	Old
Slieve	Mountain
Teer	Countryside of
Temple	Church

One or two words differing in Ireland from England

Press	Cupboard
Gardaí	The police (general)
Garda	A policeman
Fir	Gents (toilets)
Mná	Ladies (toilets)
Bruscar	Rubbish
Bord Fáilte	The Irish Tourist Board

Pronunciation

Most Irish place names are loose anglicizations of Gaelic words as already pointed out. This means that often the pronunciation is not what you'd expect... in fact hardly ever! It can be frustrating and a little embarrassing. Here are some to help you out.

Place	*Prons*
Youghal	Yawl
Dunlaoghaire	Dun'leary
Tuam	Tchoom
Laois	Leash
Abbeyleix	Abbey'leex
Oughterard	'Ookterard (as in 'look')
Nenagh	'Neenah
Inistioge	Ini'steeg
Tacumshane	Ta'cumshen
Athy	Ath'eye (as in 'high')
Clones	'Clonez (2 syllables)
(River) Suir	Shore
Naas	Naiss

Louth, Meath and Westmeath are all pronounced as if they had an 'e' on the end, as in 'seethe'.

| Ardara | Final syllable stress, Arda'ra. |

Special Places to Stay in Britain

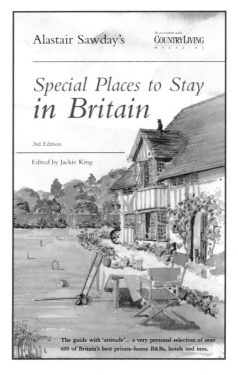

Can you afford to think of travelling in Britain without this guide? It includes over 620 fascinating places to stay in England, Scotland and Wales - each one chosen because we *like* it.

It might be the stunning, interior, spectacular setting, the amazing garden, an incredible history or a beautiful interior that won us over. A splendid breakfast beside a moat, a bedroom with heart-stopping views, a host so kind and and interesting that you may never want to leave - the book will help you discover all these things and much more besides.

Unlike other guide books that mercilessly squeeze homes and owners to fit their mould, our book allows them to do it their way - with kindness, humour and individuality.

This is the third edition of this much-loved and trusted book.
Price £12.95

Some of the wonderful places in
Special Places to Stay in Britain

From castle to cottage, from elegant to simple - a very personal
selection of places to stay for your special holiday in Britain.

Hampshire

The Guard House
The style is bright and uncluttered
and one guest room has French
windows onto a private flower-
filled courtyard. You're in the heart
of Winchester and next door is a
superb restaurant.

Tel: 01962-861514

Cornwall

The Wagon House
Charles and Mally live *on* the estate
of the Lost Gardens of Heligan!
Where better for a botanical
illustrator and a garden
photographer to set up home?
Bedrooms are simply decorated and
light floods in...

Tel: 01726-844505

Berkshire

Meadow House
Bedrooms are pretty, immaculate
and private in their own section of
this 15th-century house. Beds of
flowers and a secluded pool entice
you outside. Harriet combines care,
flair and perfectionism.

Tel: 0118 981 6005

Devon

Town House
The house is ancient, Grade II*,
and full of beautiful colour, music,
art and flowers. From your free-
standing bath you look onto the
church; the utter peace soothes the
soul.

Tel: 01404 851041

Alastair Sawday's
French Bed & Breakfast

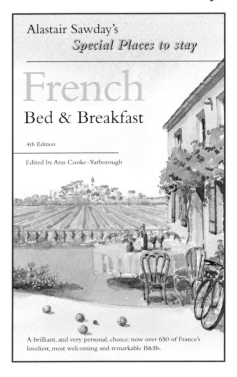

Alastair Sawday's
Special Places to stay

French
Bed & Breakfast

4th Edition

Edited by Ann Cooke-Yarborough

A brilliant, and very personal, choice: now over 650 of France's loveliest, most welcoming and remarkable B&Bs.

Put this in your glove compartment; no visitor to France should be without it!

It has become a much-loved travelling companion for many thousands of visitors to France. What a treat it is to travel knowing that someone else whom you can trust has done the researching, agonising and diplomatic work for you already. Wherever you are there will be, not too far away, a warm welcome from a French (or even English) family keen to draw you into their home and give you a slice of real French hospitality.

The selection has been honed over 4 editions, and is delectable. We can **almost** guarantee you a good time! And you will, too, save a small fortune on hotel prices.

One reader wrote to tell us that we had changed her life! Well, we don't claim to do that, but it does seem that we have changed the way thousands of people travel.

Over 660 places. Price: £12.95.

Some of the wonderful places in
French Bed & Breakfast

Spend a night in a French home, be it château, cottage, farm or manor, and discover the French in their relaxed, welcoming reality

Brittany
Les Mouettes
House and owner breathe quiet simplicity. There is light, air and nothing superfluous: carved pine furniture, durries on scrubbed planks, pale yellow or mauve walls to reflect the ocean-borne light, starfish and glowing pebbles to decorate. Pretty village too.

Tel: (0)2 99 58 30 41

Loire Valley
Le Prieuré de Vendanger
A splendid house, with its dormers, balconies and Victorian extravaganza, and a lively, creative couple who fill it with their disorganised elegance: antiques, modernities, Monsieur's murals and sculpture, Madame's relaxation course. They also roast coffee and cook deliciously.

Tel: (0)2 41 67 82 37

South-West France
Le Moulin de Samouillan
The owners left their London jobs in restaurant and theatre to restore this pretty mill in a remote farming region. Their combined skills mean superb food and beautiful decor. Fascinating wildlife, gardens rambling through patio, occasional meditation workshops, too.

Tel: (0)5 61 98 86 92

The Auvergne
Venteuges
Madame is the most natural, courageous sheep farmer's widow we know. If you appreciate genuine simplicity then walk or cross-country ski in this generous countryside and return to a 'cup of friendship', a gaggle of grandchildren, a dated decor and fabulous home-made food.

Tel: (0)4 71 77 80 66

Alastair Sawday's
Paris Hotels

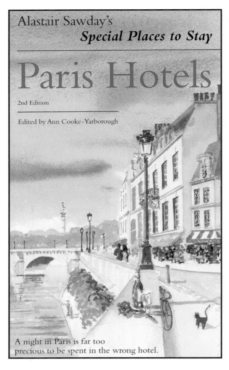

Alastair Sawday's
Special Places to Stay

Paris Hotels

2nd Edition

Edited by Ann Cooke-Yarborough

A night in Paris is far too
precious to be spent in the wrong hotel.

Things change so quickly... how on earth are you to know which hotels are still attractive and good value? Which *quartiers* are still livable and quiet? Where has the long arm of the corporate hotel world NOT reached?

Well, you are lucky to hear of this book... it will rescue your week-end! This second edition follows a successful first edition, still with just a small, select number of our very favourite hotels.

Ann Cooke-Yarborough has lived in Paris for years and has tramped the streets to research and upgrade this second edition. She has chosen with an eagle eye for humbug. Unerrringly, she has selected the most interesting, welcoming, good-value hotels in Paris, leaving out the pompous, the puffed-up, the charmless and the ugly.

Trust our taste and judgement, and enjoy some good descriptive writing. With the colour photos, the symbols and the light touch you have a gem of a book. Price: £8.95.

Some of the wonderful places in
Special Places to Stay – Paris Hotels

A night in Paris is far too precious to be spent in the wrong hotel.

4th Arrondissement
Hôtel de la Bretonnerie
A perfect marriage of ancient and modern in Paris's lovely *Marais* district, the Bretonnerie has timbers, twisty corridors and high-backed chairs set off by bold colour schemes, pretty quilts and marble bathrooms. And the people are delightful.

Tel: (0)1 48 87 77 63

5th Arrondissement
Port-Royal Hôtel
Hard by trendy Rue Mouffetard and a short walk from the Latin Quarter, the Port-Royal is simple, sober, scrupulously kempt and most welcoming. Three generations of Girauds have developed a superb sense of friendly service and outstanding value.

Tel: (0)1 43 31 70 06

6th Arrondissement
Le Relais Saint Germain
A most attractive and... un-hotelly hotel combining discreet luxury and definite personality, original timber frames and modern works of art, antique furniture and fine bathrooms. Each print is individually chosen, each client individually cared for.

Tel: (0)1 43 29 12 05

7th Arrondissement
Hôtel du Champ de Mars
Behind that pretty façade is one of the most carefully decorated little hotels we know, where blue and yellow coordinates give a cosy, country-house feel to the intimate rooms. Leafy Champ de Mars and the Eiffel Tower and right here, and it isn't expensive.

Tel: (0)1 45 51 52 30

Special Places to Stay in Spain & Portugal

The guide that takes you to places that other guides don't reach!

We've combined our discoveries in Spain and Portugal into this one remarkable book.

Put together by an editor who lives in Spain and who has deep knowledge of the culture, the people, the food and the landscape, you can trust this book.

If you want to stick to well-trodden routes, we'll tell you about the most charming places to stay. If you're feeling adventurous, we'll take you high in the hills or to the heart of the two countries and introduce you to people and places that few know of.

Country houses, beach-side hotels, religious buildings, all of them selected because they, and their owners, are special. We have found authenticity, character, charm and value in every corner of Spain and Portugal.

Third edition available June 1999, £10.95

Some of the wonderful places in
Special Places to Stay in Spain and Portugal

Discover undiscovered Spain, explore unexplored Portugal - and stay in our hand-picked hilltop castles, cosy cottages, country estates, historic townhouses.

North Spain

Hotel Aultre Naray

A beguiling manor house built at the turn of the century and cradled in by the green hills of Asturias. Designer-mag elegance, kind hosts and wonderful walks close by.

Tel: 985840808

Aragon

La Torre del Visco

A mediaeval farmhouse at the heart of undiscovered Aragon. Your hosts are retired and welcoming, the food is memorable and good taste and comfort permeate every corner of the house.

Tel: 978769015

Andalusia

Palacio de Santa Inés

Plum opposite the Alhambra this sixteenth century palace has been restored with care, flair and an open cheque book. A delectable blend of traditional Spain and creature comfort.

Tel: 958222362

Alentejo, Portugal

Hotel Convento de Sào Paulo

Swap hair-shirt for bath robe and sleep in what were the cells of the brothers of the Paulist Order. Six centuries of history and 600 acres of estate help make this one of Portugal's loveliest hotels.

Tel: (0)66 999100

Alastair Sawday's
Special Walking Holidays

Do you enjoy walking, and drool over the kind of properties we feature in our books? Do you enjoy real farmhouses more than modern hotels, breathtaking countryside more than frenetic cityscapes, regional cooking more than fast food?

If so, why not experience things feet first and join our travel company's Special Walks?

We have run tours since 1984 and this new programme includes our favourite European areas and two special holidays in South India and Sri Lanka. The tours are for 6-9 nights and cost about £800 (not including flights). All holidays will combine:

*   Wonderful properties run by friendly and interesting hosts

*   Charming and knowledgeable local guides who generally live in the areas and know its best-kept secrets

*   Walks of varying lengths so you may walk as much or as little as you like (6-12 miles a day)

*   Fantastic fresh food; mouth-watering picnics

*   Small groups of like-minded people (minimum 6, maximum 14)

And of course your luggage will be transported for you.

For more details please complete the following coupon and send it to us: Alastair Sawday's Tours, 44 Ambra Vale East, Bristol BS8 4RE

....

Name: .... Age: ....

Address: ....

....

Tel no: .... Fax No: .... E-mail: ....

Which areas are you interested in? (please circle): Andalucia, Spanish Pyrenees, The Lot, Provence, Burgundy, Dordogne, Tuscany, Umbria, Italian Lakes, Ireland, Romania, Austria, Norway, South India, Sri Lanka

Others:...

Dates I prefer: ....

Friends who may also be interested: ....

ORDER FORM for the UK. See over for USA.

All these books are available in the major bookshops but we can send them to you quickly and without effort on your part. Post and packaging is FREE if you order 3 or more books.

	No. of copies	Price each	Total value
French Bed & Breakfast		£12.95	
Special Paris Hotels		£8.95	
Special Places to Stay in Spain & Portugal		£10.95	
Special Places to Stay in Britain		£12.95	
Special Places to Stay in Ireland		£10.95	
Add Post & Packaging: £1 for Paris book, £2 for any other, **FREE** if ordering 3 or more books.			
TOTAL ORDER VALUE			

Please make cheques payable to Alastair Sawday Publishing

All orders to: Alastair Sawday Publishing, 44 Ambra Vale East, Bristol BS8 4RE
Tel: 0117 929 9921. (Sorry, no credit card payments).

Name

Address

Postcode

Tel   Fax

If you do not wish to receive mail from other companies, please tick the box ☐   IRE2

ORDER FORM for USA.

These books are available at your local bookstore, or you may order direct. Allow two to three weeks for delivery.

	No. of copies	Price each	Total value
French Bed & Breakfast		$19.95	
Special Paris Hotels		$14.95	
Special Places to Stay in Spain & Portugal		$19.95	
Special Places to Stay in Britain		$19.95	
Special Places to Stay in Ireland		$19.95	
Add Post & Packaging: $4 for Paris book, $4.50 for any other.			
TOTAL ORDER VALUE *Please make cheques payable to Publishers Book & Audio*			

All orders to: Publishers Book & Audio, P.O. Box 070059, 5446 Arthur Kill Road, Staten Island, NY 10307, phone (800) 288-2131. For information on bulk orders, address Special Markets, St. Martin's Press, 175 Fifth Avenue, Suite 500, New York, NY 10010, phone (212) 674-5151, ext. 724, 693, or 628.

Name _____

Address _____

_____

_____ Zip code _____

Tel _____ Fax _____

REPORT FORM

If you have any comments on entries in this guide, please let us have them.

If you have a favourite house, hotel or inn or a new discovery in Ireland, please let us know about it.

Please send reports to: Alastair Sawday Publishing, 44 Ambra Vale East, Bristol BS8 4RE, UK.

Report on:

Entry No _____ New Recommendation ☐ Date _____

Name of owners or hotel/B&B

Address

Tel No

My reasons for writing are :

My name and address :

Name

Address

Tel:

INDEX OF NAMES

INDEX OF PLACES